WHAT'S HERE:

USE IT TO:

Discuss goals and plans of work with council staff, using the diagrams as jumping-off points.

Help all staff and volunteers understand the benefits that Girl Scouting promises to girls.

Familiarize yourself and others with the journeys and available resources.

Create customized approaches to serving girls. It's all here: ideas for events, retreats, kick-offs, and series!

Offer start-up ideas to service units and maximize the potential of the shop as an information hub.

Share information about Girl Scouting in a fun way with parents, volunteers and partners.

DIVE INTO THE JOURNEYS: SNAPSHOTS

Familiarize yourself and others with the journeys by reading these actual excerpts from the adult guides.

STARTING THE CONVERSATION
How Journeys Can Help You

MOBILIZE PARTNERS

- Leverage the journeys' timely themes to attract partners who can bring expertise to girls. For example, try reaching out to environmental groups, outdoor recreation stores, or local farmers to support *It's Your Planet — Love It!*

- Create a pool of experts who agree to be available to volunteers by doing hands-on science experiments with girls at troop meetings, guiding an outdoor adventure, serving as an expert guide on a field trip, and so on. (There are lots more ideas in the adult guides!)

Journeys can help with everything we do!

PREPARE VOLUNTEERS

The adult guides weave together the theory and practice of the Girl Scout Leadership Experience. This gives adult volunteers a "learning by doing" experience. Talk to volunteers about how they can apply what they learned from journeys to other activities in Girl Scouting.

CUSTOMIZE PROGRAM

Journeys provide a platform to build activities tied to outcomes, instead of creating everything from scratch. Use the packaged national curriculum, then customize locally, based on your pathways and membership plans. The journey books are loaded with examples about how to do this.

TAP THE POWER OF SERVICE UNITS

Journeys provide unified themes and activities. Use them to rally the whole Girl Scout community! When all Girl Scouts in the area are using journeys, it's easier to create bigger (and more fun!) events that engage a diverse group of girls.

TELL THE GIRL SCOUT STORY

- The journeys give you a great story to tell because they tie Girl Scouting to the most relevant topics of our day (i.e., locally grown food in *Sow What?* or the status of women and girls in *GIRLtopia*).

- If you're a member of the council staff, don't forget that the fund development team can use this story when they're talking to potential funders.

RECRUIT AND RETAIN MEMBERS

The Journeys content can be customized to create events and series that excite and engage girls. This book offers ideas to get you started—check them out here:

- Pages 22–23: ideas about strengthening recruitment and retention for troops, plus ideas for getting more parents and families involved.

- Pages 24–29: ideas for attracting more teens with series based on the journey themes.

Think National, Act Local

National and Local: Complementary Roles

National Role: Provide a consistent, national leadership foundation for all Girl Scouts and their volunteers.

National

Local

Local Role:
Deliver the national program by educating volunteers. Add local flair by leveraging community resources, topical experts, and partners.

As a result, girls will:
- Gain the promised benefits (15 leadership outcomes)
- Experience the power of girls united around a common purpose
- Have access to unique opportunities in their local communities

STARTING THE CONVERSATION
Planning with Pathways

WHO NEEDS WHAT?

By focusing your program plan on your membership goals, you'll have a guidepost for all the decisions you make about how to best use your time and resources. For example, volunteers guiding a group of Brownies in their *WOW!* journey might love "roving experts" who can visit every troop in their area and offer fun science experiments about water. Result: stronger programming delivered through troops actually reaches more girls than an event—and in a more sustainable way! Ambassadors, on the other hand, might crave the opportunity to get together at special events on *Justice (It's Your Planet—Love It!)*. What kind of support can program provide to help service units run these types of events?

Girl Scout Pathways is the strategy for recruiting and retaining more members by matching grade level interest and availability with sustainable options for participation. Girl Scouting will increase membership by increasing the options available for girls and adults and creating the systems to support and sustain growth.

The diagram on the opposite page is a look at how girls—and volunteers—want to belong to Girl Scouting. It is a road map to the future, grounded in research to understand how best to give girls what they want in the way they want it. This view illustrates "targeted marketing," a way to help us reflect the needs and wants of our membership, prioritize our many opportunities, and focus our limited resources.

Though this may not be exactly true for every council, the bold strokes are:

- Troop and camps are especially important for recruiting and retaining young members.

- As girls get older, their lives and their interests become more multi-faceted. Travel, series, and events can help growing girls broaden their horizons while staying connected to Girl Scouts and their sisters around the world. In the future, girls will be able to participate through a virtual pathway as well.

No matter what pathway a Girl Scout chooses, she'll benefit by using the journey to explore the three keys of leadership. See pages 22–31 for ideas about how to use journeys in many pathways.

Grades

K	1	2	3	4	5	6	7	8	9	10	11	12
Troop												
			Camp									
					Series							
									Events			
						Travel						
				Virtual								

THE BIG PICTURE: WHY IT MATTERS
The Power of Girls Together

Achieving Our Mission

When thousands of girls across the country share a core national experience, they enjoy being part of something bigger than themselves, they have fun, and their voice gets louder and their influence gets stronger. They can see for themselves what the world looks like when girls get together to make the world a better place and what it feels like when they make a difference in their world.

Here's what will start to happen in regions across the country as more and more girls go on a journey!

Calling All World Changers

When girls at every grade level say that it's their world and they're going to change it, amazing things can happen! For example:

- What if Ambassadors advocated for girls around the world to have the opportunity to learn to read?

Here's the story we are telling!

8

- What if Seniors launched an exhibit to display their artwork showing what GIRLtopia looks like to them? What if they make it a region-wide art show? What if they put their art online, and it went viral so that people all around the globe started thinking about a perfect world for girls?

- What if Cadettes *amazed* every middle school in the country with Peacemaker Kits? (Well, OK, start with every middle school in the county!)

- What if Juniors used storytelling to share the Power of One, Team, and Community with everyone in their classrooms?

- What if Brownies "went ELF" and spread the news about the three Leadership Keys they learned about on their Quest?

- What if Daisies introduced everyone in town to their flower friends— and what they stand for? (The Law!)

- What if *everyone* started seeing the impact of Girl Scouting?

Pretty amazing, right? Keep reading for lots of ideas about how to make it happen.

Girl Scouting builds girls of courage, confidence, and character, who make the world a better place.

THE BIG PICTURE: WHY IT MATTERS
The Girl Scout Leadership Experience

Girl Scouting's promise to girls is stated in the mission: *Girl Scouting builds girls of courage, confidence, and character, who make the world a better place.* The diagram below shows how Girl Scouting fulfills the mission.

By taking a quick walk through this diagram and explanation of the Girl Scout Leadership Experience, you'll see how activities, processes, and outcomes all need to work together to achieve the intended impact on girls' lives. For more help, check out the interactive, online overview: Girl Scout Leadership Experience (aka "Ask Sophia"). You'll find the link right on the home page at www.girlscouts.org.

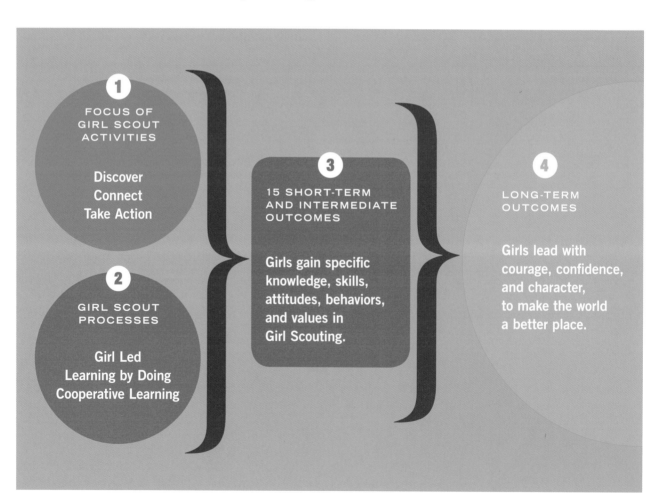

1
FOCUS OF
GIRL SCOUT
ACTIVITIES

**Discover
Connect
Take Action**

2
GIRL SCOUT
PROCESSES

**Girl Led
Learning by Doing
Cooperative Learning**

3
15 SHORT-TERM
AND INTERMEDIATE
OUTCOMES

**Girls gain specific
knowledge, skills,
attitudes, behaviors,
and values in
Girl Scouting.**

4
LONG-TERM
OUTCOMES

**Girls lead with
courage, confidence,
and character,
to make the world
a better place.**

FOCUS OF GIRL SCOUT ACTIVITIES

In Girl Scouting, girls engage in activities that help them discover themselves and their values, connect with others, and take action to make the world a better place. These are Girl Scouting's "three keys to leadership."

 GIRL SCOUT PROCESSES

It's not just what girls do, but how they are engaged that creates a high-quality experience. All Girl Scout activities are designed to use three processes that make Girl Scouting unique from school and other extracurricular activities. When used together, these processes—Girl Led, Learning By Doing, and Cooperative Learning— ensure the quality and promote the fun and friendship so integral to Girl Scouting.

 15 SHORT-TERM AND IMMEDIATE OUTCOMES

When girls do activities that are intentionally based on the three keys to leadership and that use the processes, they gain the benefits Girl Scouting promises, as described in the 15 leadership outcomes. (This is Girl Scouting's "Theory of Change.")

 LONG-TERM OUTCOMES

Ultimately, girls demonstrate these leadership skills and values as they fulfill the Girl Scout mission.

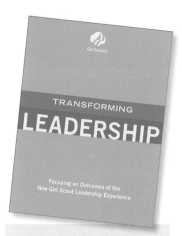

LEARN MORE ABOUT LEADERSHIP

If you're interested in learning more about how girls become leaders in Girl Scouts, check out the benefits (aka outcomes) we promised them. The outcomes are listed by Girl Scout grade level in *Transforming Leadership*. You can download the English version at www. girlscouts.org/research/pdf/ transforming_leadership.pdf or get the Spanish version at www.girlscouts.org/ research/pdf/transforming_ leadership_spanish.pdf.

JUMP START:

The leadership journeys are created to provide volunteers with activities that are already intentionally based on the outcomes and processes. As volunteers use the sample sessions in the journeys, they engage girls in the fun themes while having their own "learning by doing" opportunity with the Girl Scout Leadership Experience. That means volunteers can apply what they learn about activities, processes, and outcomes to everything else they go on to do with girls. So, journeys are an important way to engage Girl Scouting's nearly 1 million volunteers in providing a consistent national leadership experience to girls!

Discover

1 Girls develop a strong sense of self

2 Girls develop positive values

3 Girls gain practical life skills

4 Girls seek challenges in the world

5 Girls develop critical thinking

+

Connect

1 Girls develop healthy relationships

2 Girls promote cooperation
and team building

3 Girls can resolve conflicts

4 Girls advance diversity in
a multicultural world

5 Girls feel connected to their
communities, locally and globally

+

Take Action

1 Girls can identify community needs

2 Girls are resourceful problem solvers

3 Girls advocate for themselves and
others, locally and globally

4 Girls educate and inspire others to act

5 Girls feel empowered to make
a difference in the world

=

Leadership

THE BIG PICTURE: WHY IT MATTERS
The Three Keys of Leadership

Discover. Connect. Take Action.

It's not a slogan, motto, or catchphrase!

It's a simple and elegant definition of leadership, developed by the Girl Scout community.

How do these three keys of leadership play out?

DISCOVER SELF

INSTEAD OF THIS:	IT'S THIS:
"Discover how to make a T-shirt."	"Discover a value you care about enough that you want to put it on a T-shirt!"

CONNECT WITH OTHERS

INSTEAD OF THIS:	IT'S THIS:
"Connect at 8 p.m. for a pizza party."	"Have a pizza party where girls meet new people, expand their network, and do some team-building, too!"

TAKE ACTION TO MAKE THE WORLD BETTER

INSTEAD OF THIS:	IT'S THIS:
"Take Action by doing the latest dance moves."	"Take Action by starting a dance club to inspire younger girls to 'live healthy'!"

Discover. Connect. Take Action.

Nearly 4 million members use this approach to leadership. It changes the world!

THE BIG PICTURE: WHY IT MATTERS
Talk About Impact

Check out some of the specific examples of what Girl Scouting does for girls, listed on page 40. They are all based on one or more of the 15 leadership outcomes for girls.

Everyone wants these benefits for girls! Parents, principals, funders, and partners all want to hear more about the impact Girl Scouting has on girls' lives. Here are a few tips for telling that story, consistently and nationally, generating increased awareness about what Girl Scouting is really all about!

- Drill into "one row" of "one grid" in Transforming Leadership. For example, look at the Discover Outcome "Girls develop positive values" on page 49 of *Transforming Leadership* (and shown here on the opposite page). Use the information in that row to give a specific example of how Girl Scouting benefits girls. Talk about an activity, but tie it to a result. For example: "When Girl Scout Brownies go on our Quest journey, they are having fun solving a mystery, while they are also practicing using values of the Girl Scout Law—in Girl Scouts and at school and home, too. So, you'll be able to start observing how Brownies talk about 'right and wrong' choices and take responsibility for making good choices on the playground."

- As you know, real-life stories about real-life Girl Scouts are best! So you can use this same approach: what activities the girl did, how they impacted her, and how that ties to one or more of Girl Scouting's leadership outcomes.

- For more examples about how activities benefit girls when they use the Girl Scout Processes (Girl Led, Learning By Doing, and Cooperative Learning), check out the examples in the adult guides. You'll find the "Seeing Process and Outcomes Play Out in the Journey" section helpful. Samples are right here in this booklet on pages 50–97.

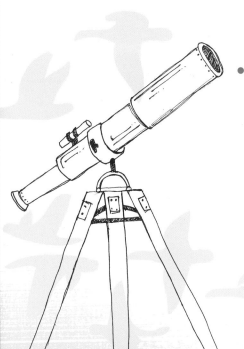

TRANSFORMING

LEADERSHIP

Focusing on Outcomes of the
New Girl Scout Leadership Experience

TRANSFORMING LEADERSHIP

DISCOVER OUTCOMES

Girl Scout Brownies u
and use their knowled

DISCOVER OUTCOMES	BY GRAD Girls...	
Girls develop a strong sense of self: Girls have confidence in themselves and their abilities, feel they are able to achieve their goals, and form positive gender, social, and cultural identities.	positively ide linguistic, rac	...ke about being a girl. recognize how their characteristics make them unique (e.g., when drawing a picture of themselves, a girl can say, "I am Korean, and I speak Korean and English").
	have increased confidence in their abilities.	express pride in their accomplishments when speaking with others.
Girls develop positive values: Girls form their beliefs and values based on the Girl Scout Promise and Law, learn to consider ethical aspects of situations, and are committed to social justice and community service and action.	begin to apply values inherent in the Girl Scout Promise and Law in various contexts.	explain how they will take responsibility on the playground, at home, and at school.
	are better able to examine positive and negative effects of people's actions on others and the environment.	explain the difference between right and wrong choices. provide alternative choices to actions that harm the environment (e.g., throw plastic bottles in recycle bin, not in trash can).

THE JOURNEYS: AN OVERVIEW
How To Start Your Journey

Here's what to suggest to volunteers (or staff!) who want to get familiar with journeys.

HOW TO GET STARTED WITH THE JOURNEY BOOKS

- **Go online at** www.girlscouts.org/gsle, then watch and listen as a guide takes you on a 10-minute tour through the **Girl Scout Leadership Experience.** The tour illustrates how each component is part of a well-researched, powerful, and change-making experience for girls. Notice too the summaries of each journey that pop up when you click on "journeys."

- **Choose a journey.** There are now two series of journey books (and one to come!):

    It's Your World—Change It! (Theme: Advocacy)

    It's Your Planet—Love It! (Theme: The Environment)

    It's Your Story—Tell It! (Theme: Creative Expression— out in December 2010)

- Read the **girl journey book**—just for the pleasure of it and to get an overview of the journey's theme.

- Use the **sample sessions** in each adult guide to bring journeys to life. Excerpts are included here on pages 50–97. Check out the journey maps at www.girlscouts.org/program/journeys/maps for ideas about how to tie other Girl Scout activities to journeys.

WHAT'S IN EACH ADULT GUIDE

The adult guide has everything you need for your journey. It includes:

- explanations of journey themes
- sample sessions
- tips for encouraging girls to choose and complete activities
- tips for making sure the Girl Scout Leadership Experience is girl-led
- ideas for Take Action projects
- steps for earning the awards

LEADERSHIP ESSENTIALS 24/7

Leadership Essentials Online, a 45-minute online learning session, introduces volunteers to the use of journeys books within the Girl Scout Leadership Experience. Because the learning session is available online 24/7, volunteers can engage in it at their own convenience. (Note: Leadership Essentials Online is interchangeable with the face-to-face version of Leadership Essentials, so volunteers can choose to use one or the other as they prepare to partner with girls.)

Link to Leadership Essentials Online: http://training. girlscouts.org

The adult guides include plenty to do during your Girl Scout year. But remember, you do not have to do everything exactly as laid out in the books. You can add or subtract sessions as needed. However, if you're super busy (and who isn't?), you can rest easy knowing that the adult guide will give you a clear plan for each session of your year—you don't have to change a thing!

Q. WHAT ORDER SHOULD GIRLS DO THE JOURNEYS IN?

A. There are no rules. Do them in any order you want!

INVITE GIRLS TO CUSTOMIZE!

Before girls even open their journey books, ask what the journey's theme means to them. Maybe the theme ignites a discussion (or even debate!) that helps the girls chart their course for the year. Probe to find out what the girls are most interested in accomplishing and enjoying over the year. This is your chance to encourage girls to dig deeper:

Notice there are planning sheets in the adult guides to help you do this.

- Can they organize and plan a trip to find out more about the topic?

- Are there events at service units or councils that tie into their interest? If not, maybe they can start one!

- Can the girls find an expert in the field to invite to their meetings?

- Which badges can the group work on to deepen their skills in this particular area?

Check out the adult guides for more tips about customizing each journey.

HAVE FUN ALONG THE WAY AND CELEBRATE!

Now step back and watch how the girls, with your knowledge, support, and guidance, have **enormous fun and a rewarding experience.** Take pride as girls earn **exciting new awards!** Enjoy the ceremony ideas provided in the journey books or encourage girls to create their own.

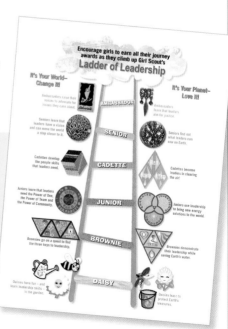

BUILT-IN AWARDS

As girls advance through the Girl Scout levels, they'll be progressing up the ladder of leadership awards. All the steps to earning the awards are built right into the girl books and the adult guides.

TIP: Make copies of the leadership ladder—found in the Ready-to-Use Handouts section of this book—to show girls and their families all they'll accomplish while having fun in Girl Scouts.

THE JOURNEYS: AN OVERVIEW
It's Your World—Change It!*

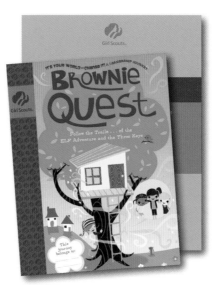

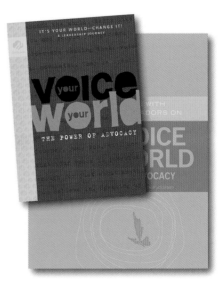

Find the fun in gardening with Amazing Daisy and the flower friends. You'll read an exciting story and learn all about making things grow!

Go on a Brownie Quest—led by the Brownie Elf herself! You'll learn all about the three keys to leadership and how to change the world with your Brownie friends.

A fashion-savvy spider named Dez will show you how you and your friends can combine your own power into team power and then use it to generate community power.

When you go on this journey, you'll find your way through the twists and turns of relationships, learning how to deal with pesky friendship problems and how to be a true friend to others.

Imagine a perfect world for girls! Create that vision as an art project, then take action to make it real. Leaders, after all, are visionaries!

How often have you seen a problem and thought, "Why isn't someone doing something about that?" This journey gives you a way to be that someone, using your networking, planning, and communication skills.

*Los libros de la serie *Es tu mundo, ¡cámbialo!* para Daisy, Brownies y Juniors también están disponibles en español.

It's Your Planet—Love It!

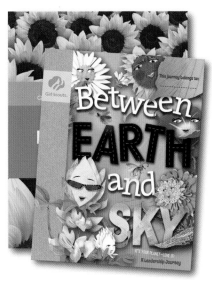

You'll join your flower friends for a cross-country road trip in their special flower-powered car! As you travel the country, you'll learn to use your own special skills to help people and Planet Earth.

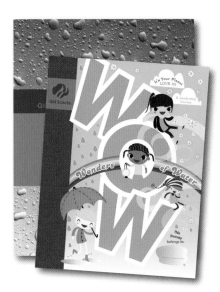

The Brownie friends and Brownie Elf enjoy some wonder-filled adventures as they invite you to explore the Wonders of Water—take a pledge to protect water and inspire others to follow your lead.

You'll find tons of energizing stuff to make and do in these pages—plus, Dez, the fashionista spider, is back to help you figure out life "off the grid."

You'll use all five senses as you clear the air—your own and Earth's! You'll inspire others to act for air and end up making an impact on Earth—and its atmosphere.

What makes a real happy meal? You'll find out as you explore food issues, scope out your own "food print," and even try out some tasty recipes. You may get some ideas for career choices, too!

Justice—for Earth and its inhabitants — we all know what it is. Why is it so hard to achieve? Maybe justice needs a brand-new equation—your equation. As you go on this journey, you'll also be networking and getting new ideas for college and careers.

Coming in December 2010: *It's Your Story—Tell It!*

THE JOURNEYS: AN OVERVIEW
Journey Maps

What makes a great Girl Scout year? Earning badges, hiking and camping, taking field trips, selling cookies, and enjoying Girl Scout traditions. Now you can tie all that together with a choice of two leadership journeys and a third journey soon to follow.

Go online at www.girlscouts.org/program/journeys/maps. You'll find a series of interactive maps (one for each grade level). As you move your mouse over the maps, pop-ups will appear with ideas about tying Girl Scout activities to each journey. These are just suggestions to get you started; have fun coming up with your own. **After all, it's your journey—customize it!**

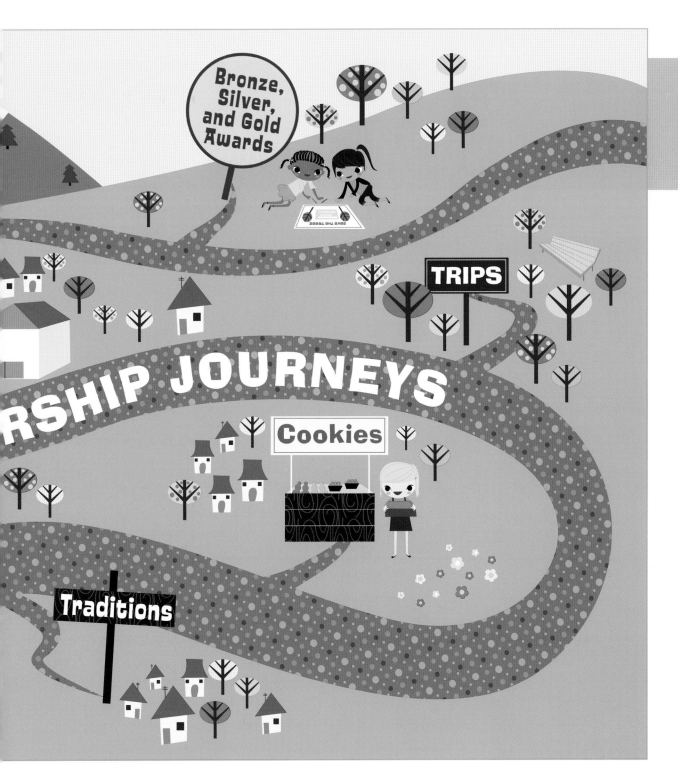

Bronze, Silver, and Gold Awards

SAVE THE TREES

TRIPS

RSHIP JOURNEYS

Cookies

Traditions

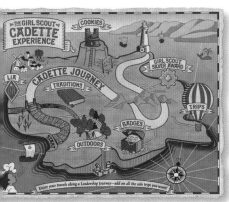

IDEAS FOR USING JOURNEYS
Kicking Off with Families

Your council, girls, and volunteers can have lots of fun as you play with journey themes to customize the content to use in many ways. This section offers a number of examples to get you started and to spark more ideas.

CREATE A KICK-OFF FOR DAISIES

Troops are an especially important pathway for Girl Scouting's youngest members—and their families! Make registration or "getting started" gatherings into a real event by adding fun activities and showcasing ways for families to get involved. Here are some ideas about using journeys to build excitement, interest—and membership! At your kick-off event:

- Start with a song ("I'm a Girl Scout Daisy...").

- Pull out one or two short excerpts from the stories in the Daisy journey books. Invite teen Girl Scouts, fun-loving parents, or any story lover to read or act out the scenes.

- Add to the fun: Take photos of girls and their families with their favorite flower friends. Maybe ask a few questions as gentle conversation starters: Why does your family love the value that flower represents? Where are each of the flower friends from? Where's your family from?

- Tell girls and their families how the things they'll do as Daisies relate to the story in their journey books. Here's a simple message you can use: The flower friends are taking off in their petal-powered car in *Between Earth and Sky!* In the same way, the Daisies are taking off on an adventure that will give them a head start on science as they explore nature. Along the way, they'll also learn how to get along with others!

CREATE A KICK-OFF FOR BROWNIES

The Brownie friends, with the help of Brownie Elf, are exploring the *Wonders of Water* (*WOW!*). In real life, the Brownies are going to become experts on the science of water—and the importance of protecting it. Plus, they are going to learn some "Ways of Working" that will really WOW you! At your kick-off event:

- Get your cameras out! Can someone dress up as Brownie Elf and pose for pictures? How about Grandma Elf?

- Create "blow up" posters of the snapshot pages (78–79 of this booklet) and set them up on easels. Family members can easily check out what their girls will be doing. Maybe parents, cousins, aunts, and uncles will see a session where they could help out!

- Use the information and special handouts in the adult guides to keep families connected to the action throughout the journey. More involved families mean more support for volunteers and increased awareness about how Girl Scouting benefits girls!

- Create a concluding ceremony that lets families know how important it is that girls have started earning Girl Scouting's leadership awards. Encourage everyone to sign up for the next level of Girl Scouting!

INVOLVE FAMILIES

Use the worksheets built right into the adult guides of the Daisy, Brownie, and Junior levels to let families know what the journeys are all about. Flip to this page:

IT'S YOUR WORLD— CHANGE IT!

- Daisy pp. 16–17
- Brownie pp. 13–16
- Junior pp. 17–19

IT'S YOUR PLANET— LOVE IT!

- Daisy pp. 33–35
- Brownie pp. 31–35
- Junior pp. 18–19

TROOP TIPS

Most of Girl Scout's youngest members enjoy being in troops. Using these ideas to engage the whole family helps keep troops strong.

IDEAS FOR USING JOURNEYS
Keeping It Short and Sweet

JUMP START JUNIORS AND CADETTES

Bring girls together for fun opportunities to dig into journey themes—and even to earn some of the journey leadership awards or participation mementos. As you consider these examples, you are likely to think of many more ways to tie award earning into your journey kick-offs.

- **Camp-Out, Lock-In, Sleepover:** Engage Girl Scout Juniors in a "Survivor-like" adventure related to *Get Moving!* as they see how little energy they can use during the course of a weekend or an overnight. Add some of the "energizing" snacks and crafts featured in the girls' journey books. Top it all off with a chance to talk to an expert guest about interesting ways to save energy. There you have it—The Junior Energize Award!

- **Wide Games:** Wide games are a wonderful Girl Scout tradition that encourages girls to explore several different activities. Here's an example of using this approach to run an event for Cadettes that culminates in them earning their "Interact" leadership award from the *aMAZE!* journey:

  Check out the Interact Challenges chart on pages 12–15 of the girl's *aMAZE!* book. Note that the chart lists specific relationship challenges, the pages in the book that deal with the skill required for that challenge, and a blank space for girls to write down what they did.

  Girls are asked to do three out of the nine challenges to earn their awards. Set up activity stations for the challenges you think will be most interesting and viable for a "wide game" event plan.

  As the event wraps up, it's always great for girls to show what they have learned and why it matters to them by talking about it, writing in a journal, drawing on a mural, and so on. (Reflection also helps with "Learning by Doing"!) So borrow a tip from the journey approach and incorporate a fun sharing opportunity into a closing award ceremony!

ADD TO THE CHALLENGE

If you can attract diverse Cadettes who don't all know each other, they can really get creative accomplishing some of the challenges right on site!

CREATE A SHORT SERIES FOR JUNIORS AND CADETTES

Girls have more to do as they grow up. Try this approach for busy fifth- or sixth-graders and their families:

- Identify parents, friends, or relatives who are willing to volunteer for eight weeks. (You can also split that in half, with one pair of volunteers guiding the first four weeks, and a second pair guiding the next four weeks.)

- Let families know that the girls can enjoy an eight-to-ten week leadership journey. They'll have a ton of fun learning and get a lot of Girl Scout essential experiences and values condensed into a two-month participation option!

- Choose whichever Junior or Cadette journey theme is of greater interest to the girls.

- By following the adult guide, the journey volunteers can coach girls to earn important Girl Scout Leadership badges and have fun with classic Girl Scout traditions along the way, too. Would families like to add on a trip? A craft project? There are ideas for those sewn into the journey guide, too.

- Plan a closing ceremony so families can see all the practical skills and values (Girl Scout Law) that girls have experienced. Have fun displaying examples of what girls learned and explored.

- Don't forget to use the closing ceremony to invite families to register for another "eight-to-ten week" episode of Girl Scouts next year. The next journey awaits!

- When planning for the series, consider the cost of membership, journey books and awards, snacks, meeting materials, volunteer guides, and add-ons like trips or crafts.

TWEAK IT!

Girl Scout families and potential volunteers are busy! This idea can also be used as a template for creating a short series for other levels, based on your membership plans.

IDEAS FOR USING JOURNEYS
Creating a Weekend Retreat

AMAZE CADETTES: WEEKEND RETREAT

Here's an example of "mixing and matching" journey sample sessions to create different ways to do the journey, depending on the time and setting.

Friday Night

As girls arrive, they can snack, listen to music (ask them to bring their "friendship playlists"), and have fun making Peacemaker Kits (**pages 39–40 in the adult guide**).

> Talk a little about the theme: Navigating the maze of relationships in our lives! Collect "relationship skills" for their Peacemaker Kits. (You might like to use some of the fun messages on **pages 4–7 of the girl books**.)
>
> Enjoy an icebreaker: try "Beneath the Surface" from **page 31 of the adult guide**. Wrap up by inviting girls to check out the ideas about stereotyping on pages 21–23 of their books and add a tip or an idea to their Peacemaker Kits.
>
> Make a team agreement. See **page 35 of the adult guide**.

Saturday Morning

> In small teams, girls create and share their own "mazes" of relationship ups and downs. See **pages 32–33 of the adult guide**.
>
> Wrap up by inviting the girls to check out the Interact Challenges on **pages 12–15 of their books**. Which challenge would they like to take? Maybe something that relates to what they put in their mazes? Anything they can do while during the retreat weekend? If they do three, they earn their Interact Award!

Saturday Lunch

> After eating, how about some get up and move around time! Depending on where you are, now's the time for a hike or perhaps a maze-like obstacle course the girls navigate with partners. Or maybe now's the time for a visiting expert who teaches *dancercise* to a global beat . . . girls will know best!

TWEAK IT!

Although this example focuses on Cadettes, you can use the same technique to create events for any grade level.

TIP:

Extra late-night energy? Show movies, sing songs, or tell stories that focus on the theme of friendship—or try one of the other fun ideas on **pages 32–37 in the adult guide**.

Saturday Evening

Check in on the Team Agreement—are we living up to it? What does our answer say about our people skills? Something more for the Peacemaker Kits!

Wide-Game Style: Choose a variety of "people skillbuilding" ideas from the adult guide and organize stations so that girls have a chance to rotate and practice what's most important to them. Below are a few ideas—you'll find many more in the adult guide. And don't forget the quizzes and other activities in the girl books!

Wrap up by giving girls time to add what they've learned to their Peacemaker Kits and do some of their Interact Challenges!

Think ahead to the "Where Do You Stand" exercise on **pages 52–53 of the adult guide**. Do girls want to add some scenarios of their own?

Sunday Morning

Start the day with some active fun. Try one of the friendship games on page 51 of the adult guide—or some other games suggested by the girls!

Check in on the Team Agreement. Any dramaramas overnight? Something to learn? Do the girls want to change or add on to the Team Agreement?

Do "Where Do You Stand" on pages 52–53 of the adult guide. Now what else can girls think about adding to their Peacemaker Kits?

Sunday Afternoon—Closing

Use "How Do Relationship Skills Impact the World" and "Who Is a Real Leader" on pages 72–73 to get the girls involved in thinking big about linking the relationship skills they've explored to examples of leadership skills that make the world better.

Close by inviting girls to create a little ceremony to share some of the ideas they have put in their Peacemaker Kits—and earn the Peacemaker Award (plus, the Interact Award, if they have completed the challenges).

TIP:

When you create events, take a look at the "Snapshot of a Journey" in each adult guide. This tool helps you see, at a glance, what experiences you most want to "mix in" to meet girl interest and need. (The Snapshots are all gathered in the back of this booklet for you, so you've got them in one easy place! See page 50 for *It's Your World—Change It!* and page 74 for *It's Your Planet—Love It!*)

ADD IT ON

If girls want to go on and earn the Diplomat Award from *aMAZE!*, consider planning a second weekend retreat and inviting younger girls to attend on Sunday afternoon. The Cadettes could then spend Saturday preparing a workshop on people and friendship skills, such as coping with bullies and using "I Statements." They can educate and inspire the younger girls on Sunday—along with enjoying some of the fun and games they have enjoyed!

IDEAS FOR USING JOURNEYS
Focusing on Teen Interests

GOING FURTHER

Some girls may be so enthusiastic that they want to do more than one event on this topic. Let them know they are also now one-third of the way to earning the "Visionary" leadership award pin. Does anyone want to move into a series to continue toward the award? Are there girls in troops who want advice about completing the steps back in their troop?

Or, if you are offering a few events related to the same journey theme, you could plan and promote them as "come to all three and get the keepsake."

CREATE AN ART EVENT FOR SENIORS

Sometimes girls are intrigued by a journey theme, but don't necessarily want to go through all the steps to earn the journey leadership award. You can still create fun events—and the journey "keepsake" bracelets and necklaces offer a fun way to give girls a tangible way to show that they participated in the event.

Create fun events by thinking of as many different ways as possible to build on the journey theme and expand some of the activity possibilities. Take *GIRLtopia*, for example:

Perhaps you want to plan an event for Seniors that will give them the opportunity to use art to illustrate their vision of a perfect world for girls. Maybe the girls can set up a gallery space to display their art . . . perhaps some girls want to collaborate on a mural . . . you might have a budding filmmaker who wants to create a *GIRLtopia* video and organize special showings . . . or a photographer who wants to record everything that's been done . . . and you could very well have a group of future publicists and event planners who want to get the word out and make the show an evening to remember! Can the girls contact local women artists who would be willing to offer advice, encouragement, or inspiration—or maybe even display their own related work?

The artwork could be unveiled to parents, the community, younger girls—and the Seniors could each take the stage to talk about their vision of *GIRLtopia*. At the end of the event, you could present the girls with *GIRLtopia* patches or necklaces to remember this special experience.

VISION
possible
lead
dream
respect
justice
create
imagine
powe

CREATE AN ISSUES SERIES FOR AMBASSADORS

Many teens want to make the world a better place, but they're busy, busy, busy—too busy, they think, to add Girl Scouts to their to-do list. What if your Girl Scout council or some service units offered a one-week "Justice Academy" during school break for 11th and 12th graders?

- Start by reading the "sample sessions" of the adult guide. You'll see how girls can earn the Sage Award by journey's end.

- Since *Justice* has ten sessions, you can tailor your academy so that you cover "two sessions" per day, including a closing ceremony.

- Add a visit with a local expert—there are examples in your adult guide.

- Along the way, you can build on some of the ideas offered in the girl and adult books and provide girls opportunities to explore green careers, use art to make a visual of "(in)justice," and enjoy some of the "nest and soar" activities.

- Finish by giving girls ideas about how to describe what they learned when they fill out college applications or go on interviews!

As each series wraps up, be sure to tell girls, their families, and schools about other upcoming series they can return for—this year or next. Think about incentives to get them to sign up right away—could they get a discount if they register early? Get their next journey books ahead of time?

When planning series like this one, consider the costs, starting with the basics: the cost of membership, journey books and awards, meeting supplies, some healthy snacks, a trip, and a closing ceremony. Consider too, how the series can be sustainable. Perhaps, for example, volunteers can "audit" with the goal of replicating the series. Perhaps partnerships can be developed in each region so that every teen Girl Scout can participate.

A BIGGER WORLD

This kind of event benefits Ambassadors because it meets their developmental needs:

- Meeting experts
- Networking
- Exploring careers
- Expanding their world
- Thinking big

It also takes the pressure off individual volunteers if you can support the series from service unit or council levels.

A FEW MORE IDEAS

Why stop at *Justice*? Use this example to think about all the other series that are possible, based on journeys as the core curriculum. How about:

- A *Your Voice, Your World* Forum?

- A *GIRLtopia* Retreat Week?

- A *Sow What* Institute every Friday afternoon in spring? (What a fun—and delicious—time to enjoy local foods.)

IDEAS FOR USING JOURNEYS
Taking It to Camp

You don't have to leave journeys behind when you head outdoors! In fact, getting away from it all on a hike or camping trip is a great way to get girls immersed in some of the journey themes in every series.

It's Your Planet—Love It!

You'll quickly find that there are many ideas about enjoying the great outdoors tucked right into the girl books and adult guides in the *It's Your Planet—Love It!* series. After all, loving nature is generally the best motivator for protecting it! So get the Daisies hiking and observing all that grows at camp, involve the Brownies in the water issues, offer the Juniors an "off the grid" adventure, invite Cadettes to enjoy "a square inch" of silence as they *Breathe*, get the Seniors checking the soil and preparing a meal of locally grown food, and have the Ambassadors do the math as they consider the footprint on a weekend at camp.

It's Your World—Change It!

This journey might not be as obvious, but it's easy to use the *It's Your World—Change It!* series at camp, too! Whether planning a day at camp for younger girls or a weekend or longer for older Girl Scouts, here are some ideas to get you going.

DAISIES: Invite Daisies and their families to a day at camp. Have fun with activities in *Welcome to the Daisy Flower Garden* like "What's In the Bag?" (on page 68 of the adult guide) and "Secret Garden Stuff" (on page 73). Take a moment to say the Girl Scout Promise and Law together and enjoy a round of "Sandy's Song for Girl Scout Daisies" (on page 75). Depending on time and interest, perhaps girls and their families can do a simple Take Action project that improves how things are growing at camp. Got an imaginative crew? Make up characters (along the lines of the flower friends) for some of the flora and fauna found at camp. Get everyone involved in creating an adventure for these friends.

BROWNIES: Brownies have their Quest Maps from *Brownie Quest*. How about a chance to learn to follow a map of a Girl Scout camp or trail? Consider "Going ELF: Search to Discover the Values of the Girl Scout Law" at camp (see page 47 of the adult guide). And how about a focus on teamwork with a special Brownie Team Agreement (see page 61 of the adult guide) for camp time?

JUNIORS: Juniors doing *Agent of Change* could come with a "herstory" to share or even act out (page 16 of the girl book). Or they can enjoy this time together to make up their own "power" story, with an outdoor twist (page 68). While telling stories, how about making up a list of funny things "Dez Says" about camp? Don't forget to practice the power of team—with an obstacle course the girls can invent at camp (page 36).

CADETTES: Camp provides freedom from usual cliques and routines. That makes it a great space to engage Cadettes on *aMAZE!*, using the "Where Do You Stand" exercise (pages 52–53 of the adult guide). After trying out some of the scenarios, give girls time to partner up and come up with some of their own.

SENIORS: *GIRLtopia* invites girls to envision the perfect world for girls. What better place to start than the "mini world" of a weekend at camp? Use the "Shared Visions" (page 39 of the adult guide) and "What's Our Ideal Group" (page 45) to get started. Add girls' imaginations and go from there! Time outdoors can also be great inspiration as girls "illustrate" what the perfect world for girls looks like through photography, watercolor, or other art media.

AMBASSADORS: Girls at the end of high school have so much going on. How about clearing the calendar for a weekend away from it all? Try these exercises from *Your Voice, Your World* for a great weekend: "Discover the Many Moods of You" (page 47) and "Discover Your Inner Child" (page 55). Don't forget the gourmet S'mores (page 24)! While sitting around the campfire, it might be nice to talk about the timeline of women who have advocated throughout history. What entry will the Ambassadors make?

IDEAS FOR USING JOURNEYS
Real-life Stories

> "The adult guide helped us structure our meetings and our year."

Donna Schneiderman
Brownie and Junior adult volunteer
Brooklyn, NY

At the year-end ceremony (for *Brownie Quest*), the girls talked about the steps involved with the first, second, and third keys, and about what the lock was. One girl who I didn't think was paying much attention had the most articulate things to say. Her mother was just beaming.

I say to the girls, you'll never forget being a Girl Scout. When I was a Brownie, we played games, we made an art project, we did the Brownie circle. We never did this level of community support. If I remember the things that we did as a Brownie, I can't imagine what these girls will remember.

Toni Hutchins
Brownie adult volunteer
Hessel, Michigan

As I was first looking through the *Brownie Quest* adult guide, I said to my daughter how nice it was that the girls [in the story] were different and that they all worked together. That's when my daughter said she wanted to do the journey. She wanted to start right away. You wouldn't know it to look at her, but she's autistic. We like it that Girl Scouts accepts everybody no matter what they are or who they are.

Our group meets every week. Last year, we did eight Try-Its. I noticed you can earn four awards in seven sessions by doing the journey. So if we do four within the first two months, that will be a big jump start for us.

The book has recipes and activities. It's easy to read, and the colors are eye-catching. The way the characters are drawn is current to what girls like now. Girls like fairies and Tinkerbell, little characters with wings, so I think the Brownie Elf is appealing and captures their interest.

Anne Bennett
Cadette adult volunteer
Columbus, Ohio

My girls are very focused on environmental issues, especially air quality, so our journey has been girl-driven rather than me-driven. One of the things I like about the journey book is that it's hands on. My girls are always saying, "We don't want to sit around and talk. We want to do something." It's been a challenge to find more hands-on activities, and *Breathe* seems to have a lot of them. Tonight we're doing the second session. The girls are looking forward to making the eclairs and the lotion, and then using them to explore the senses. And they really enjoyed the noise-making in the first session. A lot of them have MP3 players and headphones and they use their earplugs to get away from their younger siblings, so they could connect with that. It was so funny. There was a lot of noise going on!

"I'm glad it's easy to use because we are a large troop, and I don't have time to plan."

SPREAD THE WORD
Take It to the Neighborhood

FUN IS IN!

Just because Girl Scouting is focused on benefits to girls, it does not mean fun is out! A contest for the best journey-themed "add-on activity" at each level might be just the thing to ignite imaginations among girls and volunteers. Also consider pulling together holiday parties, dances, and picnics based on the journey themes.

Great things happen for girls at the neighborhood level! Here are a few helpful hints for busy service unit volunteers.

READING CLUB FOR VOLUNTEERS

Invite volunteers to get together by level and by chosen journey. (All the adults using Brownie *WOW!* in one corner, all the adults on Junior *Agent of Change* in another, and so on.) Take thirty minutes for everyone to familiarize herself with a chapter or two of the girl book and adult guide. Then spend some time discussing ideas for the meetings with girls. If volunteers enjoy this, invite them to schedule other times to read, talk, and trade ideas.

KEY MEETING

Girl Scouting's three keys to leadership apply to volunteers, too! The more adults understand the three keys, the more confident they will be as they guide girls on journeys. Notice that the introductory section of every adult guide features a page or two of questions that coach adults about how to apply the three keys. Give volunteers an opportunity to use these pages to discuss what the three keys mean to them. (This would also be a good time to use the online "Girl Scout Leadership Experience" [aka "Ask Sophia"].)

NETWORK FOR TAKING ACTION

Every journey invites girls and their volunteers to meet new people and explore new aspects of community life as they consider how they will Take Action to make a difference. Service Units can boost volunteer confidence by pooling ideas about people and places that can be tapped for community projects. Perhaps an adult in the Service Unit can even volunteer to maintain an "idea and expert bank" for girls and volunteers to use.

CRAFTY OPTIONS

For many Girl Scouts, making things is an important tradition; it is encouraged in the adult guides. Round up the adults and teens who love crafting and have a brainstorm based on journey themes. Then share the ideas with volunteers in the unit. Take it further: see if the local craft store will give discounts for supplies. Or what about holding a Service Unit "craft in"? Everybody comes together to make something symbolic of their journey!

RETENTION TIP: USE THE LIA!

The Leadership in Action Award is built right into the journeys to involve Cadettes in mentoring Brownies. The benefit? Brownies love to be inspired by middle school girls, and Cadettes love to take the lead with younger girls.

Link Cadettes on the *aMAZE!* journey with Brownies on the Quest so the girls can "change the world" together. And link Cadettes enjoying *Breathe* with Brownies on *WOW!*—they are both essential to "loving the planet!"

Results?

- *Cadettes are happy and earning LiA!*

- *Brownies enjoy learning from Cadettes.*

- *Brownies and Cadettes are more likely to stay in Girl Scouting.*

- *Brownie volunteers are thrilled to have assistance.*

- *Girls, volunteers, and their neighborhood experience the power of girls together!*

Find the LiA online and also in these adult guides: *Brownie Quest:* page 17, *Breathe*: page 20, and *WOW!*: page 36.

TRIPS

Who doesn't enjoy hitting the road? Will a few adults in the Service Unit volunteer to investigate trips that relate to journey themes? There are ideas in the guides, and girls and volunteers probably have plenty more!

END OF JOURNEY CELEBRATIONS

Each adult guide offers ideas for celebrating all that girls have experienced on their journey. Encourage all girls at each level to join together for a really big celebration! A multi-grade-level event gives girls, families, and community partners a taste of the themes explored from Daisy through Ambassador.

HONOR ROLL

Create a roster of girls of all levels who earn their journey leadership awards. Will your local newspaper publish it with a few examples of the projects girls created? How about schools? Will principals, teachers, or perhaps the PTA highlight the girls' accomplishments?

JUMP START

Give next year's volunteers opportunities to hear from this year's experts—the volunteers who have guided girls on journeys. Encourage "experts" to share ideas about field trips and other options that helped bring the journey to life.

SPREAD THE WORD
Show the Fun!

Share the excitement that is waiting for girls inside every Girl Scout journey! You are welcome to copy and share the handouts on pages 40–48 or download them at www.girlscouts.org/program/journeys. Here are some other ideas to get the word out and invite girls and volunteers to join in on the fun!

PACK IT UP AND PASS IT 'ROUND: RESOURCE KITS

Resource kits that can be passed along from troop to troop (or used at different events) make it easy and fun for girls and volunteers to get into journeys. Consider creating resource kits that include some activity supplies (turn to the first page of each sample session in the adult guides for a materials list). If possible, add thematic props (for example, funky glasses to help envision *GIRLtopia* or a colorful ticket to *Get Moving!*). Encourage girls and volunteers to add notes and suggestions to the kit before passing it along. For example, they could tell the next group of girls about what they learned, how they made a difference in the community, or how they put together a fun trip or party based on the journey theme. Girls and volunteers might even like to create a "journey journal" to hand off to the next troop!

TAKE IT ON THE ROAD: TRAVELING DISPLAYS

You can reach adults by organizing a journey display and taking it wherever adults gather for Girl Scout meetings or learning opportunities. Use the signage, posters, and marketing materials available on the OCN to create the traveling display. If you have online access at the meeting space, set up a computer and encourage everyone to spend some time exploring the journey maps (www.girlscouts.org/program/journeys/maps) and the interactive overview of the Girl Scout Leadership Experience and journeys (aka "Ask Sophia" at www.girlscouts.org/gsle).

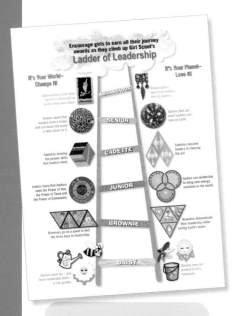

Shop Tip: Show the journey badges—maybe even make a special display!

AMP UP THE EXCITEMENT: FUN GIRL PROJECTS

What if Dez had a skirt made from recycled cookie boxes (or "old" patches)? Try creating a contest for teams of Juniors to design an "eco-friendly" outfit for her. The winning group could receive the *Get Moving!* books. Ambassadors might enjoy designing model petal-powered cars for the flower friends, then showing the cars to a Daisy group before reading to them from *Beneath Earth and Sky*.

Use the Shop

Girl Scout shops are great hubs for information about the latest national program resources that unite all Girl Scouts. Here are a few ideas that have popped up around the country:

Use Color to Get Everyone Organized: As you've noticed, the spines of the journey books provide color coding by program grade level, from bright blue for Daisies all the way up to gold for Ambassadors. Have some fun—and make the shopping trip easier for parents and volunteers—by using these tips:

- Post a color-coded Girl Scouts "growth chart" that shows the color coding for each age group.

- Color code shop shelves so that books are easier to find (for example, all Brownie resources would be on the "brown" shelf).

- Use the same color coding for announcements highlighting program activities, learning opportunities for volunteers, etc.

Make Space: Create an area where volunteers, parents, and girls can sit down and flip through the books, see the awards, or go online to check out the journey maps. Some shops have involved girls in designing a space (even a corner) with a lounge look, making it more inviting to hang out and explore what the journeys have to offer.

SPREAD THE WORD
Go Online for More

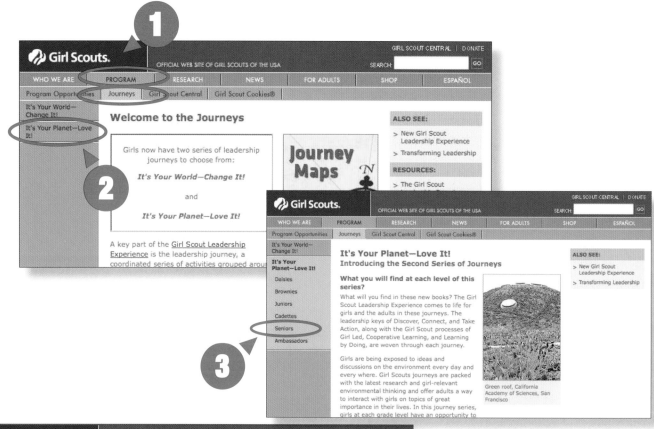

Remember, art, science, and healthy living activities are woven throughout the journeys. Check out the list of journey assets online—here's how:

1. Go to www.girlscouts.org/program/journeys.

2. Click on either *It's Your World—Change It!* or *It's Your Planet—Love It!*

3. Choose a grade level.

4. Click on "journey assets" under "downloads."

Ready-to-Use Handouts

So, you're planning events, visiting schools, talking to possible funders and community partners—wouldn't it be great to have nifty color handouts to give to people who want to know more about Girl Scouting?

The following nine pages offer just that! Feel free to photocopy them for handouts or make them into mini-posters to give away. Here's what's included:

Girls Become Leaders Through Scouting

This handout sums up what girls learn about leadership in Girl Scouts.

Ladder of Leadership

This visual guide quickly shows every girl and her family the journey leadership awards she can earn as she progresses through Girl Scouting.

The Flower Friends

Daisies and their families can learn the Promise and Law with this colorful handout.

What Will Your Girl Scout Do?

This is a great handout for a kick-off event. Get families inspired!

The Girl Scout Cookie Program

When families want to know what girls learn from selling cookies, you'll have the answer—all on one page!

Bronze, Silver, Gold

Inspire older Girl Scouts to earn Girl Scouts' highest awards.

Honor History. Make History.

Encourage girls to aim high with this visual of American women who did great things. (Be sure to point out that there's a space for a girl to add her own photo!)

It's Your Story—Tell It!

Start building excitement now—the third journey series is on its way!

Through Girl Scouting, girls become leaders who . . .

. . . can set and **achieve** goals.

. . . can use their values to **make decisions.**

. . . can create teams and **work well with others.**

. . . can **network** within their communities.

. . . can **influence others** to take a stand and do the right thing.

. . . can **run a business.**

. . . can build and enjoy friendships with people from all **different cultures** and countries.

. . . can (and do!) **act with integrity.**

. . . can **inspire others** to help their communities.

. . . can **change the world!**

Encourage girls to earn all their journey awards as they climb up Girl Scout's
Ladder of Leadership

It's Your World– Change It!

Ambassadors raise their voices to advocate for issues they care about.

Seniors learn that leaders have a vision and can move the world a step closer to it.

Cadettes develop the people skills that leaders need.

Juniors learn that leaders need the Power of One, the Power of Team, and the Power of Community.

Brownies go on a quest to find the three keys to leadership.

Daisies have fun—and learn leadership skills— in the garden.

It's Your Planet– Love It!

Ambassadors learn that leaders aim for justice.

Seniors find out what leaders can sow on Earth.

Cadettes become leaders in clearing the air!

Juniors use leadership to bring new energy solutions to the world.

Brownies demonstrate their leadership while saving Earth's water.

Daisies learn to protect Earth's treasures.

AMBASSADOR

SENIOR

CADETTE

JUNIOR

BROWNIE

DAISY

The flower friends teach Daisies the Girl Scout Law!

Hello, I'm **Sunny, the sunflower.** I'm from Great Britain, and I'm friendly and helpful.

Hi, I'm **Daisy.** I represent all parts of the Girl Scout Law. The Daisy Flower Garden is named for me—and for all Girl Scout Daisies, including Girl Scouts founder Juliette "Daisy" Gordon Low.

Hi, I'm **Lupe, the lupine.** I'm blue and honest and fair. I love to summer in Maine.

Hi, I'm **Zinni, the zinnia.** I'm spring green and considerate and caring.

Hi, I'm **Mari, the marigold.** I'm orange and "responsible for what I say and do."

Hi, I'm **Tula, the tulip.** I'm red and courageous and strong. I'm from Holland.

Hi, I'm **Gloria, the morning glory.** I'm purple, and I "respect myself and others."

Hi, I'm **Gerri, the geranium.** I'm magenta, and I respect authority.

Hello, I'm **Clover.** I'm green with white flowers. I use resources wisely.

Hi, I'm **Vi, the violet.** I'm "a sister to every Girl Scout." I'm from Australia.

Hi, I'm **Rosie, the rose.** I like to "make the world a better place."

Ordinary girls can do extraordinary things!
GS
What will your Girl Scout do?

THE GIRL SCOUT COOKIE PROGRAM

The Girl Scouts of the USA is the premier leadership organization for girls.

The Girl Scout Cookie Program is the largest girl-led business in the country and generates over $700 million for girls and communities nationwide.

Through the Girl Scout Cookie Program girls develop five essential skills:

- Goal setting
- Decision making
- Money management
- People skills
- Business ethics

For more information on the Girl Scout Leadership Experience, go to www.girlscouts.org/gsle

Journeys lead to Girl Scouts' highest awards!

Bronze
Silver
Gold

When a girl does a journey, she practices using the three keys to leadership by:

- exploring issues in her community that matter to her

- practicing teaming up

- starting a community network

- learning basic planning steps

- coming up with ideas for her Take Action project

All this leaves her poised to go on to earn the highest awards.

For more details about the Bronze, Silver, and Gold Awards, go to:

www.girlscouts.org/program/gs_central/insignia/highest_awards/index.html

Juliette Gordon Low founded Girl Scouts to help young women build self-esteem and to teach them such values as courage, honesty, compassion, and good citizenship. More than 50 million women have been Girl Scouts!

Helen Keller became deaf and blind when she was just 19 months old. Anne Sullivan, her formerly blind teacher, managed to communicate with Helen through patient teaching. Helen Keller became a prominent advocate for the needs and rights of others with disabilities.

Condoleeza Rice served as the first African-American woman US Secretary of State in the administration of President George W. Bush.

Pocahontas was a Powhatan princess who kept the peace between English colonists and Native Americans. The novel made people understand the cruelty and immorality of slavery, galvanized the abolition movement, and contributed to the outbreak of the Civil War.

Dorothea Lange was one of the outstanding photo-documentarians of the 20th century, capturing images of war, poverty, and social conditions across the country and around the globe.

Eleanor Roosevelt advocated for women, children, African-Americans, and the poor. While First Lady, she worked for the formation of the United Nations. She later served as US Delegate to the UN and policy adviser to several presidents.

Maya Lin, architectural designer and sculptor, designed the Vietnam Veterans War Memorial when she was 21. It is the most visited monument in Washington, DC, and one of the most moving memorials in the world.

Rosa Parks is known as "the mother of the civil rights movement." In 1955, she refused to give up her bus seat for a white man, triggering the Montgomery, Alabama, bus boycott, which ended with the Supreme Court ruling against racial segregation.

Hillary Clinton is the first First Lady to be elected to the United States Senate and to serve as Secretary of State. She was the first woman US Senator from New York State, and she has come the closest of any woman to being nominated for President by a major American political party.

Harriet Beecher Stowe wrote Uncle Tom's Cabin, one of the most effective pieces of reform literature ever published. The novel made people understand the cruelty and immorality of slavery, galvanized the abolition movement, and contributed to the outbreak of the Civil War.

Sonia Sotomayor became the first Latina woman to serve as US Supreme Court Justice in 2009. She achieved her position of judicial prominence by working her way up from humble beginnings.

Oprah Winfrey is the first African-American woman to own her own production company. Then she went on to create the National Child Protection Act and has given millions of dollars to causes like education, women's empowerment, orphans, and health care.

Susan B. Anthony devoted her first reform efforts to anti-slavery and to temperance. Then she spearheaded the women's rights movement. Although women did not get to vote in her lifetime, she greatly furthered the cause of women's suffrage.

Dolores Huerta, one of America's foremost labor leaders, co-founded the United Farm Workers. She led the struggle for collective bargaining rights, unemployment insurance, and immigration rights for farmworkers, and helped thousands of their children obtain services.

Harriet Tubman was a runaway slave who led more than 300 slaves to freedom along the Underground Railroad. During the American Civil War, she organized spy and scout networks that operated behind Confederate lines.

Your
Girl Scout
Here!

Georgia O'Keeffe was one of America's greatest artists. Her uniquely American paintings of flowers, New Mexico vistas, and urban landscapes have a lyrical modernism.

In 1960, Wilma Rudolph became the first American woman to win three gold medals in the Olympics. She overcame polio to become a record-breaking track star. She is one of the five America's Greatest Women Athletes selected by the Women's Sports Foundation.

Eileen Collins was the first American woman to pilot a spacecraft. In February 1995, she piloted the shuttle Discovery on an eight-day mission, which included the first space rendezvous with the Russian space station Mir.

Clara Barton, a teacher and nurse with a long record of humanitarian work, established the American Red Cross in 1881. The Red Cross developed into one of the nation's most enduring aid organizations. During her tenure, it aided victims of floods, famine, and earthquakes.

Rachel Carson wrote Silent Spring, an extensively researched book on the dangers of pesticide use in 1962. It is widely considered the single most important catalyst to the modern environmental movement.

Hedy Lamarr, the beautiful, talented Hollywood actress, was also the inventor of technology essential for both secure military communications and the cell phone industry.

In 1928, Amelia Earhart became the first woman to fly solo across the Atlantic. Her attempt to be the first person to fly around the world has captivated the imagination of girls across generations.

Sacagawea used her survival expertise and interpretive abilities to ensure the success of the Lewis and Clark Expedition in the early nineteenth century. She saved Clark's journals from a boat accident, preserving the history of the expedition.

Juliette Gordon Low: National Portrait Gallery, Smithsonian Institution/Art Resource, NY; Helen Keller and Anne Sullivan: ©Corbis/Bettman, Donated by Corbis/Bettman; Condoleeza Rice: Associated Press; Harriet Beecher Stowe: ©Corbis/Bettman, Donated by Corbis/Bettman; Pocahontas: English School/Hulton Archives/Getty Images; Dorothea Lange: Buyenlarge/Hulton Archives/Getty Images; Eleanor Roosevelt: ©Corbis/Bettman, Donated by Corbis/Bettman; Maya Yin Lin: ©Layne Kennedy/CORBIS; Rosa Parks: Don Cravens/Time & Life Pictures/Getty Images; Hillary Clinton: Associated Press; Amelia Earhart: FPG/Staff/Hulton Archives/Getty Images; Sonia Sotomayor: Associated Press; Oprah Winfrey: Associated Press; Susan B. Anthony: ©Corbis/Bettman, Donated by Corbis/Bettman; Dolores Huerta: Associated Press; Harriet Tubman: Time & Life Pictures/Getty Images; Georgia O'Keeffe: ©Corbis/Bettman, Donated by Corbis/Bettman; Wilma Rudolph: Mark Kauffman/Time & Life Pictures/Getty Images; Eileen Collins: NASA; Clara Barton: ©Corbis/Bettman, Donated by Corbis/Bettman; Rachel Carson: ©Alfred Eisenstaedt/Time & Life Pictures/Getty Images; Hedy Lamarr: ©Underwood & Underwood/Corbis/Bettman, Donated by Corbis/Bettman; Sacagawea: ©David R. Frazier Photolibrary Inc./Alamy

Honor History. Make History.

Your Girl Scout Here!

It's Your Story— Tell It!

Our stories say so much about ourselves—our likes, our desires, our dreams. The next set of Girl Scout leadership journeys gives girls the opportunity to tell their stories through a range of creative approaches. These journeys are designed to strengthen a girl's sense of herself and boost her capacity to seek and meet challenges in the world. And that, after all, is what Girl Scouting is all about.

Mark your calendars.

The next set of journeys arrives in December 2010!

Dive into the Journeys

Fabulous adventures await every girl and her volunteer. At the request of the Girl Scout community, we've included actual excerpts from the adult guides for *It's Your World—Change It!* and *It's Your Planet—Love It!* Use these to familiarize yourself and others with how the leadership experience, fun activities, and awards are all sewn into one ready-made guide for volunteers!

Snapshot of the Daisy Journey

SESSION 1	**Welcome to the Daisy Flower Garden** Girls meet one another, hear about the Girl Scout Promise, sample the Daisy story, plant their mini-garden, and play Daisy Circle, Garden-Style.
SESSION 2	**Buzzing Toward Girl Scout Values** Girls say hello in Spanish, recite the Girl Scout Promise, greet each other with the Girl Scout sign, water their mini-garden, and enjoy a "garden scamper"—all the while discovering how Girl Scout values are part of their daily lives.
SESSION 3	**Greetings and Friendships** Girls say hello in French, deepen their understanding of the Girl Scout Law—particularly "being responsible for what I say and do"—maintain their mini-garden, and play an "imitating nature" game. Their achievements earn them the Watering Can Award.
SESSION 4	**Good Thoughts, Good Deeds, Garden Needs** Girls say hello in Dutch and Persian/Farsi, maintain their mini-garden, brainstorm a larger planting/growing project, and play What's in the Bag—all the while deepening their understanding of how Girl Scout values play out in their lives and their community.
SESSION 5	**Doing and Growing** Girls say hello in Japanese, maintain their mini-garden, plant/grow (according to their Take Action Project), and take part in an active Secret Garden Time. Girls who carry out their Take Action Project to make the world a better place earn the Golden Honey Bee Award.
SESSION 6	**Celebrating the Law with a Garden Party** Girls say hello in a language of their choice, reflect on their Take Action Project, and say and explain the meaning of the Girl Scout Law. For their achievements, girls are awarded the Amazing Daisy Award and rewarded with a garden party.

NATIONAL LEADERSHIP OUTCOMES

		AT THE DAISY LEVEL, girls...	RELATED ACTIVITIES	SAMPLE "SIGN" When the outcome is achieved, girls might...
DISCOVER	Girls develop a strong sense of self.	are better able to recognize their strengths and abilities.	Sharing in the Daisy Circle and Garden Story Time discussions	make positive statements about their abilities or demonstrate to others what they can do (e.g., "I was a good friend to Luna today").
	Girls develop positive values.	begin to understand the values inherent in the Girl Scout Promise and Law.	Garden Story Time (all sessions)	identify actions that are fair/unfair, honest/dishonest in various scenarios.
		recognize that their choices of actions or words have an effect on others and the environment.	Garden Story Time and the Take Action Project	give an example of when their actions made something better for someone else.
	Girls gain practical life skills—girls practice healthy living.	gain greater knowledge of what is healthy for mind and body.	Healthful snacks learned through the garden story	name behaviors that contribute to good health (e.g., eating fruit, getting exercise).
CONNECT	Girls promote cooperation and team-building.	begin to learn how to work well with others.	Mini-garden planting (begins in Session 1 and continues throughout)	name something about themselves that helps them work well in a group (e.g., "I listen well").
	Girls feel connected to their communities, locally and globally.	are better able to identify people and places that make up their community and understand their various contributions.	Take Action Project (Sessions 5 and 6)	identify people who provide services in their communities (e.g., doctors provide medical care, teachers provide education).
TAKE ACTION	Girls can identify community needs	gain increased knowledge of their communities' assets	Take Action Project brainstorming	name people/places they consider helpful and valuable in their communities.
	Girls educate and inspire others to act.	are better able to assist peers and seek help from them.	Take Action Project and Garden Party Celebration	respond to requests for help/assistance with actions or words.

Seeing Processes and Outcomes Play Out in Daisy Flower Garden

Girl Scout processes and outcomes play out in a variety of ways during team gatherings, but often they are so seamless you might not notice them. For example, in Session 1 (page 40-43), the Daisies share about themselves as they participate in a discussion following their Garden Story Time, and then take part in creating their own mini-garden. The call-outs below show how the Girl Scout processes and outcomes make each of these activities into learning and growing experiences for girls—and up the fun, too! Throughout *Welcome to the Daisy Garden*, you'll see processes and outcomes play out again and again. Before you know it, you'll be using these valuable aspects of Girl Scouting in whatever Daisies do!

FROM SAMPLE SESSION 1

Garden Story Time

Introduce the girl characters in the Daisy story by reading the short bios of each one, pausing at the end of each to ask a question or two to spark the girls' thinking. (Story-related questions are featured in the girls' book and in various Story Time tips in this guide—but feel free to ask your own.)

Aim to engage all the girls in the discussion. You might first read a question and offer an answer of your own. Say something like, "In this story, the girls live near an old garden. Let's think about where we live. I'll start. I live in an apartment on Spring Street, just two blocks from the train station." Then say something like, "Now let's go around our Daisy Circle so each of you can share an answer to this question. Maria, let's start with you. Where do you live?" If a girl doesn't have an answer, move the conversation along with some helpful prompts. Or switch to a new question; say something like, "Where is your favorite place to play outdoors?" After the girl answers, offer a positive comment, such as: "Thank you, Maria. How nice that you _____ _____."

By introducing the flower friend characters in the Daisy story, girls begin to understand the values inherent in the Girl Scout Promise and Law, and work toward the **Discover Outcome, Girls develop positive values.**

When all the girls have answered, recap what they've done:

- Let them know they've all just shared something special about themselves, such as where they live or where they like to play.

- Encourage them to write or draw their responses in their book and to share their book with their families.

- Remind them that they will share more about themselves at future Girl Scout sessions.

Then, let the girls know you will now read them the first chapter of the Daisy story.

After the reading, ask the girls the garden-related questions that follow Chapter 1 of the story:

- Do you have a garden at home or near where you live? What makes it special?

Explain to the girls that not everyone has a garden. Some people live in apartments and might not have room for a garden. Instead, they might have a window box or a pot of flowers.

Have the girls look at all the flowers, plants, animals, birds, and insects pictured in their books. Ask them: If you could have any kind of garden you wanted, what would be in it? Move around the Daisy Circle and invite all the girls to say what they might want in their garden. Let them know that they will have a chance to create their own garden right in their books

> These discussion questions are excellent examples of engaging Daisies in a **Girl Led** way as girls answer a "W" question about where they live and freely express their ideas, feelings and opinions about their own or ideal gardens.

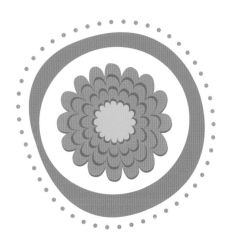

Snapshot of the Brownie Journey

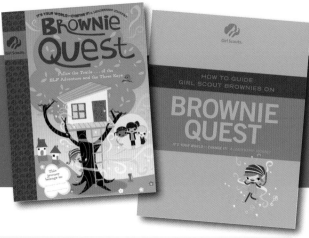

SESSION 1	**Discovering . . . • You:** Brownies join in a circle and, with a ball toss, introduce themselves and name their skills and qualities. **• Values:** Brownies "go ELF" to search for values of the Girl Scout Law. **• Family:** Each Brownie heads home to discover her family's special qualities and the value of the Law that resonates most with her family.
SESSION 2	**Discovering and Connecting. . . • In the Brownie Star Circle:** Brownies share their family discoveries and join in the first Quest ceremony, earning their first key. **• By Teaming Up:** Brownies play cooperative games, then create their own Team Agreement. **• With Family:** Brownies commit to leading a healthy-living activity with their families.
SESSION 3	**Connecting and Taking Action . . . • Making a Circle Map:** Brownies explore how the "circles" of their lives grow outward: Me, Family, Girl Scouts, Community, World. **• Posting Commitments:** In the map's Family circle, Brownies post Commitment Cards noting their family's healthy-living actions. **• Caring for Community:** The Team expands its circle of caring through two stories—one real, one fictional—that serve as springboards to writing letters to a school or town official to seek a healthy-living improvement. **• Earning the Second Key:** Brownies close with the Quest's second award ceremony.
SESSION 4	**Choosing a Take Action Project • Brownie Brainstorm:** Team members consider community places where they could Take Action to make a difference. **• Brownie Team Trade:** The Team "goes ELF" while deciding on top ideas for taking action. **• Brownie Plan:** The Team talks about preparations and materials they need to Take Action.
SESSION 5	**Taking Action • Brownies Get Busy:** Depending on their project, the Team creates a skit, gathers supplies or donations, learns about a community issue, etc. **• Brownie Team Reflects:** The girls describe their project and their thoughts about it. **• ELFing It Up:** Time permitting, the Team creates "what if?" endings to "The ELF Adventure" story, sings Brownie songs, or makes a gift to swap.
SESSION 6	**Making the World a Better Place • Wrapping Up:** Brownies conclude their efforts to reach out and make an impact in their community. **• ELFing It Up One More Time:** Time permitting, the Team explores new endings/adventures for "The ELF Adventure," makes healthy treats, tries the extra puzzles and activities in their Quest books, or creates a closing ceremony. **• Meeting Juliette:** The Team considers how Juliette Gordon Low discovered, connected, and took action, and adds a note to her in their books. **• Earning the Third Key:** Brownies take part in their third award ceremony.
SESSION 7	**Unlocking the Code to Leadership: Celebration and Reflection** Wrap up the journey with cheer as Brownies find that when they Discover, Connect, and Take Action, they are leaders! They earn the Quest Award and add a "leadership commitment" card to their Quest books. Follow tips in the guide for their ceremony.

NATIONAL LEADERSHIP OUTCOMES

	AT THE BROWNIE LEVEL, girls...	RELATED ACTIVITIES	SAMPLE "SIGN" When the outcome is achieved, girls might...
DISCOVER — Girls develop a strong sense of self.	have increased confidence in their abilities.	"Discovering Me" (Session 1). "Taking Action" (Sessions 5-6).	express pride in their accomplishments when speaking with others.
Girls develop positive values.	begin to apply values inherent in the Promise and Law in various contexts.	"Discovering Family" (Sessions 1-2: Sharing values of GS Law with family).	explain how they will take responsibility on the playground, at home, and at school.
Girls gain practical life skills— girls practice healthy living.	are better at making healthy choices and minimizing unhealthy behaviors.	"What's Happening at Campbell's House" and "Leading Your Family to Health" action (Sessions 2-3).	name healthy choices they make (e.g., walking every day, choosing healthful snacks).
CONNECT — Girls develop healthy relationships.	begin to understand how their behavior contributes to healthy relationships.	"Leading Your Family to Health" (Sessions 2-3).	identify healthy/unhealthy behaviors (e.g., honesty, caring, bullying) when presented with a relationship scenario.
Girls promote cooperation and team-building.	gain a better understanding of cooperative and team-building skills.	"Team Agreement" (Session 2) and follow-up reflections on keeping agreement. "Brownie Team Trade" (Session 4).	describe ways to make projects more fun (e.g., switching roles, brainstorming, listening to each other).
Girls feel connected to their communities locally and globally.	recognize the importance of being part of a larger community.	"Caring for Community" (Session 3). Take Action Project (Sessions 5-6).	give examples of how group/ community members help and support each other (e.g., in their neighborhood, school).
TAKE ACTION — Girls can identify community needs.	develop basic strategies to identify community issues.	Creating and doing the Take Action Project (Sessions 4-6).	list things about their community that are valuable and things that could be improved.
Girls educate and inspire others to act.	can communicate their reasons for engaging in community service and action.	Creating and doing the Take Action Project (Sessions 4-6).	explain why they chose a community action project (e.g., meals to seniors, holiday gifts to needy children), how/ why it benefited others, and what they learned from it.
Girls feel empowered to make a difference.	increasingly feel they have important roles and responsibilities in their groups and/or communities.	"Caring for Community" (Session 3). Brownie Brainstorm (Session 4). Take Action Project (Sessions 5-6).	describe ways their actions contributed to bettering something (for their families, neighborhoods, environment).

Seeing Processes and Outcomes Play Out in *Brownie Quest*

Girl Scout processes and outcomes play out in a variety of ways during team gatherings, but often they are so seamless you might not notice them. For example, in Session 1 (page 46-50), the Brownies share about themselves as they participate in a lively ball toss activity, and then take part in a Quest to discover values of the Girl Scout Law. The call-outs below show how the Girl Scout processes and outcomes make each of these sample activities learning and growing experiences for girls—and up the fun, too! Throughout Brownie Quest, you'll see processes and outcomes play out again and again. Before you know it, you'll be using these valuable aspects of Girl Scouting in whatever Brownies do!

FROM SAMPLE SESSION 1

Ball Toss: Discovering Our Special Talents and Qualities

In this game, the girls discover and name some of their special talents or qualities, and then discover and appreciate what other girls bring to the Brownie Circle. Plus, they can release a little energy!

Begin by gathering the girls into a circle and welcoming them to the Girl Scout Brownie Quest.

Say something like:

- When we join in a Girl Scout Brownie Circle, we're making connections with millions of girls all over the world standing in Brownie Circles just like this one. Imagine 500,000 girls doing this same thing—you are part of this amazing sisterhood!

- Every time we create our Brownie Circle, we can imagine that it is like a giant tree house—where Girl Scout Brownies around the world belong together.

- Today, we are using our Brownie Circle as the start to our special Quest to find three keys. There are three steps we have to take to find each key. Ready for the first step toward the first key?

- The first step is to discover all the skills and talents and qualities each of us brings with us on our Quest. So, as we toss the ball around our circle, say your name and one special skill or talent or quality that you can bring into our Brownie Circle.

- I'll start: My name is _____ and I have a lot of energy, so I never give up!

As the girls toss the ball around, encourage them to describe their qualities and talents. If they get stuck, read out lines from the "Discovering Me" activity page and have the girls fill in the blanks.

Record (or ask a Brownie friend or family member to record) what the girls say. Do this inside the large star you sketched on poster board or newsprint. Label it "Discovering Ourselves." At upcoming sessions, this will be a good visual reminder of what the girls discovered about themselves at the Quest's start. Option: Invite the girls to decorate the Brownie Team star as the meeting ends or at the beginning of the next session. Then display it each time the Team meets and at a closing celebration.

When everyone has had a few turns tossing and catching, wind down by summarizing the qualities and talents the girls bring to their Brownie Circle.

Consider ending the activity with a friendship squeeze. Ask the girls to silently appreciate the qualities of the girl next to them as they pass along the squeeze.

As girls toss the ball around the circle, they develop important gross motor skills and release energy too! They are **Learning** (about others) **by Doing!** Through this activity, they are also discovering and sharing their talents and skills by expressing pride in their abilities when speaking with others. This helps them achieve the **Discover Outcome, Girls discover sense of self.**

The reciprocal nature of this ball toss perfectly demonstrates a **Cooperative Learning** activity for this age. The girls rotate through different roles (sometimes tossing, sometimes catching) and develop a sense of belonging to the group.

Snapshot of the Junior Journey

SESSION 1	**Discovering My Power** Girls have a chance to see their own strengths and powers in everyday ways and then start comparing them to those of past and present "heroines."
SESSION 2	**Great Leaders and Great Teams** Using the knowledge they've gained about the strengths and powers of "heroines," girls connect personal power to the values expressed in the Girl Scout Law. They then explore what power means in girls' lives and in society, and see their power in action. They earn their first award, the Power of Team Award.
SESSION 3	**SuperShelter-Makers** Building on their understanding of their own power and the power of past and present women, the girls explore the powers used by a team of fictional girls who, in a comic-book-style story, take action to improve their community. The girls then create their own supergirl story.
SESSION 4	**Learn, Listen, Act! Taking Idea to Action** The girls use the power of story to identify what they care about enough to take action on in their own community. They begin to see how, with team power, they can accomplish great things together.
SESSION 5	**Ready, Set, Take Action!** Reaching out into the community, the girls gather the tools and resources needed to take action for change, and earn the Power of Team Award.
SESSION 6 & 7	**Time for the Take Action Project** Combining the Power of Team and the Power of Community, girls do their Take Action Project. Then they take time to reflect on and celebrate the change they have accomplished as they earn their culminating award, the Power of Community Award.

NATIONAL LEADERSHIP OUTCOMES

	AT THE JUNIOR LEVEL, girls...	RELATED ACTIVITIES	SAMPLE "SIGN" When the outcome is achieved, girls might...
DISCOVER — Girls develop a strong sense of self.	gain a clearer sense of their individual identities in relation to and apart from outside influences.	"What Makes Me *Me*?" (Session 1) "The GS Law Meets the Heroine in Me" (Session 2)	report increased confidence in dealing with outside pressures that try to dictate their thoughts and behaviors (e.g., peer pressure, advertising, cultural traditions).
Girls develop critical thinking skills.	show greater skill in gathering and evaluating information.	"Rediscovering Herstory" (Session 1); "Who Can Mobilize the Moxie?" (Session 2); "Building Consensus: Fist-to-Five" (Session 4)	consider various factors before deciding what to believe (e.g., how credible was the source of information, is there a hidden agenda?).
CONNECT — Girls promote cooperation and team building.	are better able to initiate and maintain cooperation on their teams.	All activities in Sessions 2–4	with minimal adult guidance, apply specific strategies for promoting cooperation (e.g., listening to all ideas, rotating tasks and roles, developing shared goals).
Girls feel connected to their communities, locally and globally.	are better able to recognize the importance of knowing about and actively participating in their community groups.	"Defining Community" (Session 4); Doing the project (Sessions 5-7)	identify various sources of information for what is going on in their communities (e.g., the Internet, magazines, interviews with people).
TAKE ACTION — Girls can identify community needs.	learn to use strategies to determine issues that deserve action.	"Narrow It Down"; "Campaign for Change" (Session 4)	use community asset mapping to identify opportunities to better their communities.
Girls are resourceful problem solvers.	are better able to create an "action plan" for their projects.	"Who's Going to Do What?"; "Take Action Project Checklist" (Session 5)	outline steps, resources, and time lines and assign responsibilities for their project with minimal adult guidance.
Girls feel empowered to make a difference.	are more confident in their power to effect positive change.	Sessions 6 and 7	describe various expressions of power around them (e.g., power over others, power to do something, power with others).

Seeing Processes and Outcomes Play Out in *Agent of Change*

Girl Scout processes and outcomes play out in a variety of ways during team gatherings, but often they are so seamless you might not notice them. For example, in Session 3 (page 62-63), the Juniors develop and participate in their Opening Ceremony, and then experience and develop shared stories. The call-outs below show how the Girl Scout processes and outcomes make each of these sample activities learning and growing experiences for girls—and up the fun, too! Throughout *Agent of Change*, you'll see processes and outcomes play out again and again. Before you know it, you'll be using these valuable aspects of Girl Scouting in whatever Juniors do!

> Particularly at the Junior level, Opening Ceremonies can always be **Girl Led,** with girls taking the lead on planning and conducting the ceremony. When girls together take responsibility and team up to organize the ceremony without adult direction, this activity becomes a *Cooperative Learning* experience that also nicely fits the **Connect Outcome, Girls promote cooperation and team building.**

FROM SAMPLE SESSION 3

OPENING CEREMONY

If girls are earning the Power of One Award, you may want to start with the awards ceremony. Or you may even want to do a traditional Girl Scout opening, such as the flag ceremony. For the details of opening with a flag ceremony or to find a ceremony planner to help in creating your ceremony, visit www.girlscouts.org/program/gs_central/ceremonies/flag.asp.

Reading "SuperShelterMakers"

"SuperShelterMakers" is a story of a few Girl Scouts who have the moxie to mobilize themselves, other girls, and finally a whole community.

Feel free to add your own ideas about "the power of reading" to Dez's "pitch."

Have fun reading the comic-book story. Even if some or all of the girls have read it between sessions, try to have a shared reading experience of the story by:

- asking the girls to volunteer to take the parts—and don't forget Dez's part
- allowing some girls to be on Dez's team and offer responses to Dez's questions along the way
- staying sensitive to the girls' reading skills

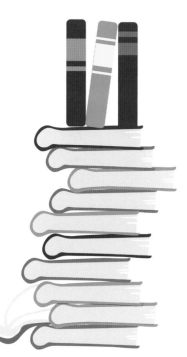

Take as long as this activity needs. Let the girls have fun experiencing the story together (which is different from reading it alone—no matter how enjoyable that is).

Begin Your Own Heroine Story

Talk informally about the "SuperShelterMakers" story—whatever in it interests the girls:

- Is there a character they especially like? Why?
- Is there anything they'd do differently?
- What do they think of Dez and her comments?
- What could have gone wrong?
- What "what ifs" can girls think of? How would they solve them?

Ask the girls for their preference: What format do they want their story to take? They can also create their story in small groups or as one large group. One way to start is to answer the "Think About It" questions related to "SuperShelterMakers" on page 67 of the girls' book. Give the girls the time they need to develop their stories in their own way.

Remember, too, that part of the joy of creating a story is the chance to tell it. Who can they tell it to? Other Juniors in the region? Younger girls? Perhaps they want to show it at their school or save it for sharing at their ending celebration.

This activity is part of earning the Power of Team Award.

The girls will form teams to create their own supergirl comic-book story or script, or any kind of visual story about taking action to make their world better. It could be a mini-play, like a TV episode, or a crazy map, a radio show, or a puppet show. Big or small, the choice is up to the girls.

Throughout the story creation, girls are also **Learning by Doing.** When girls develop and share their Heroine stories, they also uniquely demonstrate to others how to Take Action to make the world a better place. Thus, this activity is also helping girls achieve the **Take Action Outcome, Girls educate and inspire others to act.**

As the girls rotate roles in reading and experiencing the story together, this, too, becomes a **Cooperative Learning** activity. This experience also helps girls achieve the **Connect Outcome, Girls promote cooperation and team building.**

These discussion starters are a great example of how to get girls articulating their ideas and opinions about this and other stories, as well as problem solving, in a **Girl Led** way.

As girls begin to develop their own Heroine stories collaboratively in small or large groups, they engage in all three processes! The activity is **Girl Led,** since girls are offering their preferences and strategizing plans for their story formats. Beginning their own stories in smaller or large groups also makes this a **Cooperative Learning** experience that moves girls toward the **Connect Outcome, Girls promote cooperation and team building.**

Snapshot of the Cadette Journey

SESSION 1

First Impressions in the Maze Girls are introduced to the *aMAZE!* journey and: • identify possible relationship obstacles in the "maze of life" • identify peers and adults who provide key support in their lives • make choices and decisions, including a team agreement for the journey • begin exploring the impact first impressions have on relationships

SESSION 2

Navigating Friendships Girls start their Peacemaker Kits to collect the relationship skills they practice along the journey, and: • understand how stereotypes impact relationships • identify the personal qualities they bring to and seek in healthy friendship circles

SESSION 3

Cliques and Conflicts Girls identify different types of peer pressure and how it influences them, and: • practice strategies for managing peer pressure based on values • understand the exclusive and hurtful behaviors that can happen in cliques • use "I-Statements" as an important conflict resolution tool

SESSION 4

Caution: Bullies Straight Ahead Girls identify characteristics of bullying behavior and relational aggression, and: • practice skills to address bullying behavior and relational aggression • gain greater understanding of girls' roles as witnesses in bullying situations • set boundaries and develop strategies for building safe online relationships

SESSION 5

Let Peace Begin with You Girls explore the Girl Scout definition of leadership and apply it to their lives, and: • understand how leaders use relationship skills to improve the world • create and plan a Take Action Project to increase the peace in their world

SESSION 6

Improving Relationships in the World Girls plan and carry out their Take Action Project, and: • continue to connect with each other practicing relationship skills individually and as team members

SESSION 7

Toward Peace: Take Action! Girls complete their Take Action Project, and: • prepare for the closing ceremony and celebration

SESSION 8

Pass It Forward Girls evaluate their Take Action Projects, and: • reflect on their aMAZE journey and their role as leaders who inspire peace through strong, positive relationships • celebrate their accomplishments

NATIONAL LEADERSHIP OUTCOMES

	AT THE CADETTE LEVEL, girls...	SAMPLE "SIGN" When the outcome is achieved, girls might...	EXAMPLES of how the outcome plays out in this journey
DISCOVER — **Girls develop a strong sense of self.**	are better able to negotiate the effects of sociocultural factors, gender issues, and stereotyping/bias on their sense of self.	make use of strategies to resist peer pressure (e.g., communicate with confidence, take responsibility for own actions).	Sessions 1-3
DISCOVER — **Girls develop critical thinking.**	are better able to examine issues and ideas from various perspectives.	debate or discuss various perspectives on an issue they are concerned about (e.g., women's rights, global warming).	Sessions 1-3
CONNECT — **Girls develop healthy relationships.**	are able to use positive communication and relationship-building skills.	give examples of behaviors they use to promote mutual respect, trust, and understanding.	The entire journey!
CONNECT — **Girls can resolve conflicts.**	strengthen their conflict resolution and prevention strategies.	say how they manage their emotions (e.g., anger, hurt) to diffuse a conflict situation (e.g., don't lose their temper).	Taking on issues and meeting others in the community while planning and taking action.
CONNECT — **Girls feel connected to their communities, locally and globally.**	strengthen existing relationships and seek to create new connections with others in their communities.	use various ways to connect with others, locally and globally (e.g., the Internet, get-togethers, *destinations*, events).	All steps to the Interact Award
TAKE ACTION — **Girls are resourceful problem solvers.**	increasingly seek out community support and resources to help achieve their goals.	identify people/organizations in their communities to help on some aspect of their project (e.g., obtain editing guidance for media projects).	All steps to the Diplomat Award
TAKE ACTION — **Girls educate and inspire others to act.**	show increased commitment to educate others on how to better their communities.	organize a show-and-tell for younger Girl Scouts to educate them about how to be more active in community affairs.	All steps to the Peacemaker Award

Seeing Processes and Outcomes Play Out in *aMAZE!*

Opening Ceremonies should always be Girl Led, with Cadettes taking the lead on planning and conducting the ceremony. With advance preparation, girls will volunteer to sign on for active roles in such ceremonies. When girls together take responsibility and team up to develop and organize the ceremony without adult direction, this activity also becomes a **Cooperative Learning** experience that also nicely fits the **Connect Outcome, Girls promote cooperation and team building.**

This activity is an excellent example of each of the three processes in action together! As girls engage in the group discussion and corresponding exercise, they are articulating the reasons behind their decisions, sharing their opinions and debating ideas with others in a **Girl Led** manner.

Girl Scout processes and outcomes play out in a variety of ways during team gatherings, but often they are so seamless you might not notice them. For example, in Session 3 (page 51-52), the Cadettes develop their own opening ceremony and participate in an activity on peer pressure. The call-outs below show how the Girl Scout processes and outcomes make each of these sample activities learning and growing experiences for girls—and up the fun, too! Throughout *aMaze!,* you'll see processes and outcomes play out again and again. Before you know it, you'll be using these valuable aspects of Girl Scouting in whatever Cadettes do!

FROM SAMPLE SESSION 3

OPENING CEREMONY

Invite the girls to reconnect with one another using a ceremony of their choice—or jump into a friendship game.

Where Do You Stand?

This activity gives girls a chance to take a stance on peer pressure, clarifying their own values in the process. Start by inviting girls to think about times when they have been pressured or perhaps pressured others to do things that go against their values. You can use some of these points to begin:

- *We all have experiences that test our values. Do we ever trade in what we believe just so we can belong? How do we feel after doing that?*

- *We also have times that we pressure others. Why? Can that sometimes be "for their own good?" (Pressure can sometimes be for good. Can you give examples?)*

The discussion questions and corresponding Cooperative Learning exercise detailed here nicely aims girls towards achievement of three of the **Discover Outcomes: Girls develop a strong sense of self** (as they offer strategies to resist peer pressure), **Girls develop positive values** (as they clarify their own values during this exercise), and **Girls develop critical thinking** (as they debate and discuss opinions and perspectives on peer pressure). Girls respectfully listening to and trusting others in this activity helps them to achieve the **Connect Outcomes, Girls develop healthy relationships** and **Girls promote cooperation and team building.**

- *Sometimes the pressure to do something you don't want to do can be silent. Can you think of examples of silent pressure?*

- *Have you ever accomplished something you didn't think you'd be able to do, but were able to because of someone else's influence?*

Transition from the discussion by saying something like:

We are going to do an activity to push one another to explore what it feels like to stand up for our values. We really have to trust one another and uphold our team agreement for this to be meaningful. Ready?

Then, with masking tape, mark a line down the center of the room. On one end, put a piece of paper on the floor with the number 10. On the other end, put a 1. In the middle, mark a 5.

Tell the girls that you (or girl volunteers) are going to read aloud a scenario and if they think it's OK, they go to number 10. If they feel it's not OK, they go to number 1. If they're "on the fence," they go to number 5.

After each scenario is read and each girl takes her stance on the line, invite each to talk about why she stood where she did. Do any girls want to try to persuade others to stand somewhere else? Why or why not? When the girls have exhausted what they have to say, read another scenario. Some scenarios may invite more conversation than others, and you may work through a handful fairly quickly as girls become more engaged.

You might prompt the girls' conversation by asking questions such as:

What are you really saying if you go to the middle, on number 5? Are you worried about taking a stand? What are your worries? Trying to please everyone? What would help you make a decision?

A FEW SCENARIOS

I'd cancel plans with my friend if my crush asked me out at the last minute.

It's cool to disrespect your parents in front of friends.

It's important to act like you have more money than you really have.

Because this is not a straightforward discussion and asks girls to literally "stand up" for what they believe in, girls are also **Learning by Doing.** Having girls engage in an active, physical experience here will result in girls' deeper understanding of her own and others' stance on peer pressure. It will also offer her actual practice in standing up for herself that she might use in future "real-life" situations.

Snapshot of the Senior Journey

SESSION 1   *GIRLtopia*: **What's It All About?** Girls learn about the choices involved in the *GIRLtopia* journey, including the Senior Visionary Award, begin to plan and schedule their journey, and • gain an awareness of the need for a "GIRLtopia" and begin to express their visions for it • explore their values • build their understanding of visionary leadership • start to plan their "Create It" projects and think about their "Guide It"

SESSION 2   **What's on Girls' Minds?** Girls use decision-making skills to decide their approach to ceremonies, and • promote team-building by determining how to act as an "ideal group" • practice basic research skills as a way to explore community issues • enjoy "Create It" time • check in on the group's dynamics

SESSION 3   **How's Our Community Doing for Girls?** Girls review the results of their surveys, and • identify community needs through community mapping • develop their own "Girls' Bill of Rights" • continue their "Create It" projects

SESSION 4   **Choosing to Take Action** Girls brainstorm to decide on the issue and focus of their Take Action Project(s), and • practice making team decisions as they create a plan for taking action • think about possible solutions to their issue

SESSION 5   **What Would You Do?** Girls consider their values, and • practice ethical decision-making • plan their action projects • assess their progress on shared goals • have time for "Create It" and/or "Change It" projects

SESSION 6   **What Do Leaders Sound Like?** Girls continue "Guide Its" (consider topics such as "Courage" and "Promise and Law"), and • "Sound Off" on qualities of "leaders" and "nice girls" • assess their team dynamics • have time for "Create It" and/or "Change It" projects • start planning a closing celebration

SESSION 7   **How Will We Lead the Way?** Girls wrap up their "Create It" and "Change It" projects, and • reflect on leadership values • assess their team dynamics • complete plans for their closing celebration

SESSION 8   **Do I Inspire You?** Girls reflect on and evaluate their projects, and • reflect on and evaluate their group dynamics • reflect on leadership values (if not covered in Session 7) • celebrate their success

NATIONAL LEADERSHIP OUTCOMES

		AT THE SENIOR LEVEL, girls...	SAMPLE "SIGN" When the outcome is achieved, girls might...	EXAMPLES of how the outcome plays out in this journey
DISCOVER	**Girls develop a strong sense of self.**	are better able to recognize and address personal and social barriers to reaching personal goals.	make connections between societal issues (e.g., prejudice based on gender or race) and their opportunities to achieve goals	Girls learn about and reflect on the status of women and girls throughout the world.
	Girls develop positive values.	strengthen their own and others' commitment to being socially, politically, and environmentally engaged citizens of their communities.	report increased positive attitudes of social responsibility and citizenship.	Girls envision a GIRLtopia, practice ethical decision-making, create a Girls' Bill of Rights, and Take Action to move the world closer to their ideal.
	Girls develop critical thinking.	apply critical thinking skills to challenge stereotypes and biases in their lives and in society.	question assumptions behind inequities they encounter (e.g., female athletes earning less than male athletes).	Girls apply critical thinking throughout GIRLtopia.
CONNECT	**Girls promote cooperation and team building.**	strengthen their abilities to build effective teams to accomplish shared goals.	identify specific strategies for building effective teams (e.g., paying attention to interests, strengths, team dynamics). demonstrate that they can reach consensus on common goals.	Girls assess their team dynamics—team-building that strives to reach an ideal.
	Girls feel connected to their communities, locally and globally.	actively seek to bring people together in local and global networks.	give an example of organizing a local or global event that brought together diverse members of their communities.	Girls take on issues and meet others in the community in the process.
TAKE ACTION	**Girls can identify community needs.**	are more skilled in identifying their local or global communities' needs that they can realistically address.	identify community partners that can continue their project goals into the future.	Girls report considering multiple factors before deciding on the appropriateness of a project for their community (e.g., feasibility, balance of assets and needs, sustainable impact).
	Girls educate and inspire others to act.	are better at inspiring and mobilizing others to become more engaged in community service and action.	shape messages to explain the importance of taking action on an issue they care about.	Girls shape their messages in their "Create It," "Guide It," and "Change It" projects.
	Girls feel empowered to make a difference.	are better able to address challenges to their feeling of empowerment.	identify internal and/or external barriers to feeling empowered to create change.	In the GIRLtopia journey, girls learn of barriers to women and girls on a global level—and Take Action to break them down.

Seeing Processes and Outcomes Play Out in *GIRLtopia*

This activity is an excellent model of the Girl Led process, with Seniors defining their ideal journey environment—from the physical space to how their group might most effectively work together. Girls are engaged in expressing their opinions, listening to others, prioritizing and negotiating team values. This activity is also clearly a **Cooperative Learning** experience as girls apply collaborative skills to work toward a shared vision with their team. The activity moves girls toward the **Connect Outcome, Girls promote cooperation and team building.**

By answering the reflection questions that follow the group discussion here, girls engage in the **Learning by Doing** cycle. Girls also consider what they learned as an individual and as a group; together, they develop ways they'd like to modify the process in the future.

This question is an excellent example of getting girls to think critically through guided reflection. As girls learn to examine ideas from a variety of viewpoints through this and other questions, they are achieving the **Discover Outcome, Girls develop critical thinking.**

Girl Scout processes and outcomes play out in a variety of ways during team gatherings, but often they are so seamless you might not notice them. For example, in Session 2 (page 55-49), Seniors define for themselves their ideal group environment for the journey experience and later assess and reflect on the group dynamics and learning. The call-outs below show how the Girl Scout processes and outcomes make each of these sample activities learning and growing experiences for girls—and up the fun, too! Throughout *GIRLtopia*, you'll see processes and outcomes play out again and again. Before you know it, you'll be using these valuable aspects of Girl Scouting in whatever Seniors do!

FROM SAMPLE SESSION 2

What's Our Ideal Group?

In this activity, girls define the ideal environment they want for their group, and practice negotiating common values as a team.

- Ask girls to break into small groups (three or four girls) to brainstorm the behaviors and attitudes they want in their group. Give each group strips of colored paper (or luggage tags) to write their ideas on.

- Explain that this is a chance for the girls to decide what they want their group to be like. For example, in an ideal group, how do they want to treat one another? What's the best way for girls to get along? How do they want to interact with you and other adults involved?

REFLECTION QUESTIONS FOR GROUP DISCUSSION:

- *How does the environment you just described compare with other places or groups you belong to?*

- *Do you think our group's list for an ideal environment would be different if boys were a part of it? Why or why not?*

- *Can we say this list represents our group's values? (If helpful, come up with a definition for values, such as "personal beliefs that affect our attitudes and actions" or "what we would stand up for.")*

Assessing Our Team Dynamics

Using their "ideal" list, girls evaluate their own group dynamics and practice negotiating common values as a team. Remind girls that this is an opportunity to evaluate how they are doing at maintaining their own ideal group environment. Invite girls to guide both the evaluation and recording processes.

● Hang the "Assessing Our Team Dynamics" list where everyone can see it.

Let the girls decide on a ranking system (1 = not at all; 2 = some of the time; or smiley/frown faces). Then have girls rate their group environment based on each item on the list. (Be sure to label the girls' comments as being from Session 2, so they can keep track of their process/progress.)

REFLECTION QUESTIONS FOR GROUP DISCUSSION:

● *Was it easy or hard to reach a consensus as a group?*

● *Is there anything you want to change, any attitudes or behaviors, to make the group more like the ideal environment you want? Is there anything that we are not saying to each other that we need to be saying?*

● *Is being able to reach a consensus or negotiate with others an important leadership skill? Why or why not? If so, can you think of any real-life examples where a leader, either yourself or someone else, made a difference by using this skill?*

Each aspect of this activity and the reflection are **Girl Led** when girls themselves are guiding the evaluation and reflection processes.

Having girls systematically evaluate their team's dynamics is another great example of **Learning by Doing.** Here girls consider how elements of their ideal group played out or not.

This assessment is also followed by reflection questions and completes the **Learning by Doing** process. Here, girls may consider modifying their environment based on what they discovered in the evaluation so that it better meets the group ideal.

The assessment activity above and this reflection question target girls' abilities to both assess their progress and adjust their strategies as necessary. Together, these complementary activities help girls progress toward the **Take Action Outcome, Girls are resourceful problem solvers.**

Snapshot of the Ambassador Journey

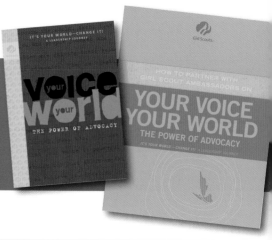

SESSION 1

Introduction, Find Your Cause Girls learn about choices involved in the journey and begin to plan and schedule their journey and • create a "girl-led" team agreement • explore the meaning of advocacy and the steps involved, and the usefulness of advocacy in their lives

SESSION 2

Community Needs and Personal Causes Girls identify their connections in their communities and • use their ideas about community needs to explore possible areas for advocacy • practice public speaking based on values of the Girl Scout Law • consider trying on a "new mood" based on a personal outlook they want to practice

SESSION 3

Tuning in on an Issue Girls explore how their efforts could cause a "ripple effect" of action on their chosen issue and • practice making realistic decisions based on their available time and, through research, break their issue down, "tuning in" to one specific angle of it

SESSION 4

Building a Network of Partners Girls assess what they have learned about their issue and then create realistic solutions they will try to advocate toward and • "harmonize" by identifying and beginning to reach out to partners who can strengthen their advocacy efforts • develop team plans to "divvy up" next steps related to working with partners and identifying the "VIPs" who can act on their proposed solution

SESSION 5

Reporting Back on Partners and Possible VIPs, and Planning the Perfect Pitch Girls assess and share progress mobilizing partners and identifying VIPs and • explore the kinds of power and influence the VIPs they have identified could have on the issue/solution • create and practice their presentation to VIPs

SESSION 6

Closing the Loop Girls assess the effectiveness of their pitch to VIPs and • create plans for next steps or "closing the loop" so that their "butterfly effect" continues (whether or not they continue advocating) • plan their own Opening Ceremony

SESSION 7

Reflect, Reward, Celebrate Girls reflect on what they have learned, felt and experienced on the journey and its impact on them and • celebrate their experience based on their plans – perhaps even "passing it on" in some way to others

NATIONAL LEADERSHIP OUTCOMES

		AT THE AMBASSADOR LEVEL, girls...	SAMPLE "SIGN" When the outcome is achieved, girls might...	EXAMPLES of how the outcome plays out in this journey
DISCOVER	**Girls develop positive values.**	act consistently with a considered and self-determined set of values.	choose educational and career goals in line with the values they consider important.	Girls' advocacy issues reflect their values and allow them to "live" their values.
	Girls seek challenges in the world.	have increased confidence to discuss and address challenging issues and contradictions in their lives and in their communities.	look for ways personal habits conflict with achieving goals that are important to them (e.g., fighting global warming).	The journey offers many challenges—reaching out to new people, speaking up, being assertive.
CONNECT	**Girls promote cooperation and team building.**	are able to promote cooperation and effective team-building in their communities.	describe how their advocacy efforts encouraged sustained cooperation among various people and/or organizations in their communities.	Girls organize partners— in team-building that may go far beyond girl-to-girl or peer teamwork.
	Girls feel connected to their communities, locally and globally.	have extensive feelings of connection with their local and global communities.	place high value on providing support for diverse members of their communities.	Girls take on issues and meet others in the community in the process.
TAKE ACTION	**Girls can identify community needs.**	are more skilled in identifying issues that balance feasibility with achieving long-term changes in their local or global communitites.	identify community partners that can continue their project goals into the future.	The first two steps to advocacy compel girls to think of root causes of a community issue. Selecting VIPs makes them consider who owns the issue and who can influence change.
	Girls advocate for themselves and others.	actively seek partnerships with other organizations that provide support and resources for their advocacy efforts.	report working with organizations that share their advocacy goals.	The whole advocacy process.
	Girls feel empowered to make a difference.	feel their projects and ideas are valued/respected by stakeholders in their local and/or global communities.	give examples of positive reports about their advocacy efforts.	The "8 Steps to Advocacy" allow girls to break down the advocacy process and feel confident at each step along the way.

Seeing Processes and Outcomes Play Out in *Your Voice, Your World*

**ELIMINATING
SPEAKER'S JITTERS**

This green box suggests
the importance of offering
Ambassador girls helpful
tips and the opportunity to
practice public speaking
for their advocacy efforts.
As girls gain and use these
skills, they move toward
the **Take Action Outcome,
Girls educate and inspire
others to act.** When girls
develop creative ways to
communicate to others, they
are engaging in an advanced
aspect of the **Learning by
Doing** process.

This fun alternative to
traditional mapping is an
excellent example of the
Girl Led process. It allows
girls to physically create and
participate in community
networks, which is a key
element of the Girl Led
process for this age group.

Girl Scout processes and outcomes play out in a variety of ways
during team gatherings, but often they are so seamless you might
not even notice them. For example, in Session 2 (page 44–46), Girl
Scout Ambassadors play Community Pretzel, a unique community mapping
game, and then reflect on what they learned. The call-outs below show how
the Girl Scout processes and outcomes make each of these activities
learning and growing experiences for girls—and up the fun, too! Throughout
Your Voice, Your World: The Power of Advocacy, you'll see processes and
outcomes play out again and again. Before you know it, you'll be using these
valuable aspects of Girl Scouting in whatever Ambassadors do!

FROM SAMPLE SESSION 2

Community Connections and the Community Pretzel

Next, suggest that the girls play Community Pretzel, a fun, physical game sort of
like Twister that will get them talking once again about the community connections
they started exploring in the first session. The girls may even want to lead this
game themselves, or they may suggest substituting another activity that gets them
thinking about their connections. Here's the basic concept for Community Pretzel:

- The girls stand in a circle within arm's reach of one another.
- The "caller" (either you or a girl) says a type of community (for example, 11th
grade or the basketball team or the French Club) and asks the girls to connect
one part of their clothing or their body with the same part of another member
of that community. For example, If you are a member of the sports-playing
community, place the sides of your shoes together. Or, if you are a member of
a religious community, touch one of your knees to a knee of another member
of that community. Girls are to remain connected throughout the game.
- Start by having the girls connect in small ways—pinkies, shirtsleeves, wrists,
ankles—so you have plenty of options to work through before you run out of
the basics like hands, feet, knees, elbows, ears, shoulders, and backs.
- By the time you get halfway down the list, you may have a giant pretzel of
giggling girls standing before you. Ask if they want you to keep going. Their
level of comfort with physical proximity and contact may be reaching its limit!

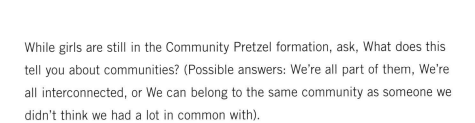

While girls are still in the Community Pretzel formation, ask, What does this tell you about communities? (Possible answers: We're all part of them, We're all interconnected, or We can belong to the same community as someone we didn't think we had a lot in common with).

After the Ambassadors untangle themselves, invite them to discuss how the Community Pretzel can be viewed as a physical representation of the group's shared communities. Did they notice how their various communities varied in size? Were they surprised by the size of any of the communities or by the members of those communities? Were there any communities they don't belong to but wish they did?

Next, steer the discussion toward advocacy:

- Ask: What does the idea of community connectedness have to do with advocacy?

- Next, give each girl a colored marker, and ask all the girls to take a turn writing what communities they are members of on a large piece of newsprint. If more than one girl writes the same community (such as Ambassadors, their grade in school, etc.), have them use arrows or bubbles to connect them.

- Then ask the girls to use a different colored marker to write the issues they have heard expressed in each community they have just noted. (Remember, they were going to do some community research ahead of this session.) The resulting "community map," which will reveal what's happening in their various communities, will aid them as they focus their advocacy efforts.

REFLECTION AND DECISION

- Engage the girls in a discussion of the reflection questions on page 47 of their book.

Guide the discussion so that girls narrow their ideas to the one issue (or a few issues, if the group has split into small teams) they will advocate for during the rest of the journey. As the team comes to a decision, encourage the girls to check in on their team agreement (from Session 1). How are they doing? Is it hard or easy to make a team decision? Why?

This activity, along with the corresponding discussion questions, demonstrates how girls make gains towards two important **Take Action Outcomes** simultaneously, **Girls feel connected to their communities locally and globally,** and **Girls identify community needs.** Through the pretzel game, girls gain a greater understanding of the many communities they belong to, as well as the interconnectedness among the different communities. Girls also identify community resources and needs through this game, which will help them choose a focus for their advocacy efforts.

This focus question helps guide the girls in group reflection and, ultimately, group decision-making around an advocacy project, thus making this activity a strong example of both **Learning by Doing** and **Cooperative Learning.** Just by weighing alternative issues and coming to a decision, girls also take the beginning steps toward the **Take Action Outcome, Girls advocate for themselves and others.**

Snapshot of the Daisy Journey

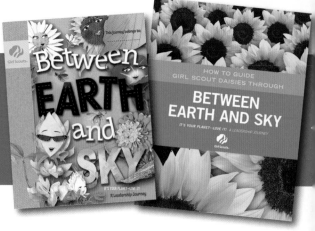

SESSION 1	**Getting Ready for the Road** The Daisies begin to express their feelings and start to understand and experience the joys of travel, especially outdoors in nature.
SESSION 2	**The Road Trip Begins** The Daisies continue to explore what makes them unique as they start to consider the feelings of their sister Daisies and expand their knowledge of shapes in nature.
SESSION 3	**You, Me, How Different We Can Be** The Daisies continue to explore their feelings and how they might differ from one girl to another. They also explore the range of colors in nature and earn their Blue Bucket Award.
SESSION 4	**Living the Law, and So Many Seeds** The Daisies explore living the Girl Scout Law through favorite flower friends and expand their knowledge of seeds and how they travel as a step to understanding how vegetation can vary around the world. The girls also try their hand at origami.
SESSION 5	**Special Skills, and Textures, Too** The Daisies continue to explore their similarities and differences as they consider the skills they contribute to their Daisy group and gain an understanding of the diversity of shapes in nature.
SESSION 6	**We Have Skills and So Do Plants** The Daisies make use of their special skills and begin to understand the special skills of plants, too. The girls also have an option to paint with natural colors made from fruits, vegetables, and other natural items, and they earn their Firefly Award.
SESSION 7	**In the Land of Milk and Cheese** The girls take the flowers friends story to a personal level by learning about how foods can affect how they feel and by tasting foods from their region. They also take a walk in nature to explore textures.
SESSION 8	**When the Flowers Meet the Trees** The Daisies choose a project idea, practice talking about it, and create visual tools for their project. They also have an option to make bark rubbings.
SESSION 9	**Protecting a Natural Treasure** The Daisies team up to protect a natural treasure of Earth and hear the final chapter of the flower friends' road trip story.
SESSION 10	**On the Road to New Adventures** The Daisies celebrate all they've learned and done along the journey! The girls also earn the Clover Award.

NATIONAL LEADERSHIP OUTCOMES

		AT THE DAISY LEVEL, girls...	RELATED ACTIVITIES (by session number or girls' book chapter/page)	SAMPLE "SIGN" When the outcome is achieved, girls might...
DISCOVER	Girls develop a strong sense of self.	are better able to recognize their strengths and abilities.	S6: Opening Ceremony, Closing Ceremony. GB: When Soon Is Better, p. 49	make positive statements about their abilities or demonstrate to others what they can do.
	Girls develop positive values.	begin to understand the values inherent in the Girl Scout Promise and Law.	S3: Story Time; S4: Opening and Closing; S10: Opening Ceremony. GB: pp. 10, 14, 20, 22, 23, 62, and 77; all women and girl profiles; Chapter 6	identify actions that are fair/unfair, honest/dishonest in various scenarios.
		recognize that their choices of actions or words have an effect on others and the environment.	S7, S8, S9: Clover Project. GB: pp. 13–14, 42–46, 50, 58, 69, 84, and 96; Chapter 6	give an example of when their actions made something better for someone else.
	Girls gain practical life skills—girls practice healthy living.	gain greater knowledge of what is healthy for mind and body.	S3: Feast of Plant Parts; S4: Story Time; S7: Story Time; S8: Snack Time. GB: pp. 53, 65, and 93	name behaviors that contribute to good health (e.g., eating fruit, getting exercise).
	Girls seek challenges in the world.	demonstrate increased interest in learning new skills.	All nature, science, art activities; S2–S6: Opening, Story; S3: Feast; S7: Story and Snack; S8, S9: Story, Clover Project. GB: Words for Wise, fact, and activity pages	ask lots of questions/make lots of observations about the world around them.
	Girls develop critical thinking.	recognize that the thoughts and feelings of others can vary from their own.	S2 and S3: Opening, Role-Play, Closing; S9: Opening; S10: Words and Deeds. GB: All differences among flower friends	make statements that show they recognize another's feelings or opinions.
CONNECT	Girls develop healthy relationships.	are better able to demonstrate helpful and caring behavior.	S1, S2: Role-Play; S4: Deeds. GB: All chapters	spontaneously offer to help someone in need of assistance (e.g., opening door, carrying package).
		are better able to identify and communicate their feelings to others.	S1, S3: Role-Play. GB: All conversations among the flower friends	express their feelings verbally rather than nonverbally.
	Girls promote cooperation and team building.	begin to learn how to work well with others.	S1, S2, S3: Role-Play, Blue Bucket Award; S4, S5, S6: Firefly Award. GB: Teamwork among the flower friends	name something about themselves that helps them work well in a group (e.g., "I listen well").
	Girls can resolve conflicts.	begin to understand what conflict is.	S1: Role-Play. GB: All mentions of Yellow Lupine and White Sweetclover: Chapter 1, p. 16; Chapter 2, p. 32; Chapter 6	give examples of conflict situations in their lives.
		learn simple conflict-resolution strategies.	S1: Role-Play, Taking a Walk. GB: Chapter 3, Chapter 6	express feelings using "I statements" when they find themselves in a conflict situation.
	Girls advance diversity in a multicultural world.	recognize that it's OK to be different.	All Sessions: Opening ceremonies. GB: All flower friends, Tatiana, and Jaz	identify characteristics that make them different from other girls.
		increasingly relate to others in an inclusive manner.	S3: Role-Play. GB: Flower friends behavior among themselves and toward others	notice when others are excluded from activities.
	Girls feel connected to their communities.	are better able to identify community people/places and understand their contributions.	GB: All women and girl profiles	identify people who provide services in their communities.
TAKE ACTION	Girls are resourceful problem solvers.	learn the basics of planning a project.	S7, S8: Clover Project	with adult guidance, make a list of resources needed to complete their project.
	Girls advocate for themselves and others.	recognize that they can act on behalf of others.	S1, S2, S3: Role-Play; S7, S8, S9: Clover Project. GB: All chapters	recognize situations when they can "make something better" for someone else.
	Girls feel empowered to make a difference.	feel their actions and words are important to others.	S1, S2, S3: Role-Play; S7, S8, S9: Clover Project. GB: All chapters	give an example of something they have done to make them feel like an important part of their group.

S=Session, GB=Girls' Book

Seeing Processes and Outcomes Play Out in the Daisy Journey

Girl Scout processes play out in a variety of ways during team gatherings, but often they are so seamless you might not notice them. For example, in Session 1 (page 45), the Daisies take part in a role-playing activity about resolving conflicts. The call-outs below show how the Girl Scout processes make this activity a learning and growing experience for girls—and up the fun, too! Throughout *Between Earth and Sky,* you'll see processes and outcomes play out again and again. Before you know it, you'll be using these valuable aspects of Girl Scouting in whatever Daisies do—from taking a romp in the great outdoors to engaging in Girl Scout Cookie Activities.

FROM SAMPLE SESSION 1

Role-Play: How Do We Settle a Conflict?

Ask the girls to volunteer to pair up and do some role-playing. The aim is to get them to move beyond simply saying how they feel, as they did in their opening ceremony, and take into consideration the feelings of others when they team up.

> This is a good example of **Cooperative Learning** as girls team up to focus on gaining conflict-management skills.

Start by giving the girls this scenario:

> *It's been raining all morning, but now the rain has stopped. You're at a friend's house, and you're trying to decide what to do. Your friend wants to stay indoors and draw pictures. You want to go outdoors and splash in the rain puddles. Neither of you wants to change your mind, but you both want to play together.*

> Though this is part of the same activity, this goal is directly aimed at the **Discover outcome, Girls develop critical thinking skills** as they work toward recognizing and considering that other people have thoughts and feelings that are different from their own.

Then explain the larger picture of what is happening:

> *When two people want to do different things and neither one will give in, it's called a* conflict.

So a conflict is when people disagree about something. They don't have to quarrel or use angry or loud voices or ugly words, but they have different views of the same situation. In this case, the two friends disagree about what they should do together.

Then ask: *What might you do to end this conflict, so you and your friend can play together and have a good time?*

Depending on how the girls respond, here are some possible hints to get them thinking toward a solution that the two friends might both agree to:

- *One of you might be nice enough to let your friend have her way and say, "Let's do what you want to do. Next time, we can do what I want to do."*

- *You might agree to do both things! You could first go splash in some puddles and then come inside, dry off, and draw pictures together.*

- *You might agree to do something else altogether, like playing games with a younger brother and teaching him something you've learned in school.*

Ask: *How does it feel to find a way to make yourself and your friend happy?*

If you have time, ask the girls to offer their own examples of times when compromising like this is a good idea.

Then say: *When you work out things like this with a friend, it's called compromising. That's a good way to get along with people. On this journey, we're going to collect good ways to talk with one another and good ways to get along. We're going to collect them all in our blue bucket—like the blue buckets we'll see the flowers riding in when we hear the story of their road trip.*

This explanation is perfectly designed to fit the **Connect outcome, Girls can resolve conflicts**, at the Daisy level. In this exercise, girls are learning the meaning of conflict and how to identify a conflict when they see one. The activity also helps girls learn basic conflict-resolution strategies.

This activity of learning various ways to compromise is both **Cooperative Learning** and **Learning by Doing.**

In a compromise, girls recognize that what they say and do affects other people so significantly that they must reconsider their position if everyone is to be satisfied in the end. This consideration and recognition of their actions on the feelings of others is aimed at the **Discover outcome, Girls develop positive values.**

Compromising, especially among friends in scenarios such as this, is an act of caring, and therefore this activity is focused on the caring aspect of the **Connect outcome, Girls develop healthy relationships.** As the very foundation of teamwork is compromise, so the **Connect outcome, Girls promote cooperation and team building,** is supported here as girls learn to work well with others through compromise.

Snapshot of the Brownie Journey

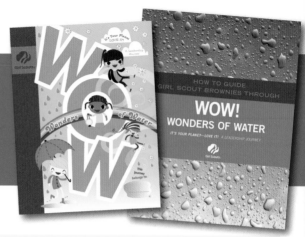

SESSION 1	**Loving Water** The Brownies begin exploring the Wonders of Water, what they LOVE about water, and why it's important to protect water.
SESSION 2	**"Green" Tea for a Blue Planet** Through a festive tea party, the Brownies learn about the water cycle. They realize that everyone on Earth shares water, and that's why it's so important to save and protect it.
SESSION 3	**Water for All** The Brownies report back on how they carried out their promises to protect water and earn their LOVE Water awards. They then engage in water-gathering and rationing activities to experience how families make do in places where clean water is scarce. This deepens the Brownies' understanding of the importance of saving Earth's water.
SESSION 4	**Teaming Up to Advocate for Water** The Brownies create a team plan to SAVE water.
SESSION 5	**Advocates Communicate!** The Brownies prepare to carry out their SAVE project as a team. They might also be learning more about their water issue through a guest visitor or even a field trip.
SESSION 6	**SAVE!** The Brownie Team advocates for saving water.
SESSION 7	**Planning to SHARE** The Brownies discuss the success of their SAVE effort and what they learned from it. They earn their SAVE Water awards and get creative as they plan to educate and inspire more people to protect water.
SESSION 8	**SHARE!** The Brownies SHARE what they've learned and how they've acted to SAVE water with others (younger kids, family members, school, community). They invite their guests to take action for water.
SESSION 9	**WOW!** The Brownies reflect on their journey—from loving water as individuals, to saving water as a team, to sharing what they know with even more people and inviting them to protect water, too. The girls receive their WOW! awards.

NATIONAL LEADERSHIP OUTCOMES

		AT THE BROWNIE LEVEL, girls...	RELATED ACTIVITIES (by session number or girls' book part/page)	SAMPLE "SIGN" When the outcome is achieved, girls might...
DISCOVER	Girls develop a strong sense of self.	have increased confidence in their abilities.	S5: Communicate It! GB: P2 and P4: WOW	express pride in their accomplishments when speaking with others.
	Girls develop positive values.	begin to apply values inherent in the Girl Scout Promise and Law in various contexts.	S1: Protecting Water and Living the GS Law; S2: Loving and Protecting Water: Continuing the Conversation; S3, S8, and S9: Opening Ceremonies. GB: P3: WOW, p. 77; P4: Mottos & Secret Words	explain how they will take responsibility on the playground, at home, and at school.
		are better able to examine positive and negative effects of people's actions on others and the environment.	S1: Thinking About Water, Protecting Water; Living the GS Law; S2: "Green" Tea; S3: Our Team WOW Map. GB: WOW Wisdom quizzes; P2: How I Use Water	provide alternative choices to actions that harm the environment.
	Girls seek challenges in the world.	are more open to learning or doing new and challenging things.	Planning and carrying out the SAVE and SHARE projects; S4: Opening Ceremony	enjoy trying new activities.
		recognize that one can learn from mistakes.		feel it is OK to make mistakes and might describe an instance in their own lives where they learned from a mistake.
CONNECT	Girls develop healthy relationships.	begin to understand how their behavior contributes to maintaining healthy relationships.	GB: p. 21: WOW	can identify healthy/unhealthy behaviors (honesty, caring, bullying, etc.) when presented with a relationship scenario.
		are better able to show empathy toward others.	GB: p. 33: WOW: Exploring People's Differences	make empathetic statements and/or report being more caring in their interactions with others.
	Girls promote cooperation and team building.	gain a better understanding of cooperative and team-building skills.	S5: Preparing to Save; S9: Gifts of Leadership	be able to identify strengths or talents that each girl brings to group projects.
	Girls feel connected to their communities, locally and globally.	recognize the importance of being part of a larger community.	S2: "Green" Tea, Talking About Tea; Send It Home: My Water Promise; S3: Team WOW Map, Building Awareness of Water in the World; S4: LOVE, SAVE, SHARE	give examples of how group/community members help and support each other.
TAKE ACTION	Girls are resourceful problem solvers.	are better able to develop a basic plan to reach a goal or a solution to a problem.	S3: Rationing Water; S4: Choosing a Save Water Project. GB: P3, WOW: Teaming and Planning to Save Water	identify two or three steps and resources (people, materials, information) needed to reach a goal or solve a problem.
	Girls advocate for themselves and others.	gain a better understanding of their rights and those of others.	S1: Thinking About, Protecting Water; S3: Building Awareness of Water; S4: Planning; S7: Earning SAVE; S8: Quiet Please	name rights people have in their schools, families, or communities.
		learn and begin to apply basic advocacy skills.	S5: Communicate It! GB: P2: WOW, p. 56	define what advocacy means and give examples of advocates in their communities.
	Girls educate and inspire others to act.	can communicate their reasons for engaging in community service and action.	S4: Heroines for Water; S7: Pass It On; S8: Educate and Inspire. GB: P1–4: All profiles of women and girls; WOW, pp. 29, 54–57, and 85; P2: No More Heavy Lifting; P4: Beach Erosion, pp. 102–103;	explain why they chose a community action project.
	Girls feel empowered to make a difference.	increasingly feel they have important roles and responsibilities in their groups and/or communities.	GB: P2: Time for a WOW, pp. 26–27; Saving and Protecting Water	describe ways their actions contributed to better something (for their families, neighborhood, environment).
		exhibit increased determination to create change for themselves and others.	S6: SAVE Project. GB: P4: WOW, pp. 100–101; My WOW Awards, pp. 107–108.	give examples of when they succeeded in making positive change for themselves and others.

S=Session, GB=Girls' Book, WOW=Time for a WOW!, P=Part

Seeing Processes and Outcomes Play Out in a *WOW!* Activity

Girl Scout processes play out in a variety of ways during team gatherings, but often they are so seamless you might not notice them. For example, in Session 5 (page 79), the Brownies plan their SAVE project. The call-outs below show how the Girl Scout processes make this activity a learning and growing experience for girls—and up the fun, too! Throughout *WOW!*, you'll see processes and outcomes play out again and again. Before you know it, you'll be using these valuable aspects of Girl Scouting in whatever Brownies do—from earning a Try-It to planning a trip.

FROM SAMPLE SESSION 5

Preparing to SAVE

Now the girls will likely need time to create materials or presentations for their team's SAVE effort. They might be designing signs to hang in a school about not running water longer than needed, practicing how to ask people to use refillable water bottles, or making a presentation to ask everyone in their neighborhood to check for leaks.

This is an example of the **Girl Led** process. The girls are taking the lead on deciding what their presentations will be and what their signs will look like for the SAVE effort. That they are making their own signs is also an example of **Learning by Doing.**

Practicing is an example of **Learning by Doing.** This activity is also an example of the **Take Action outcome, Girls educate and inspire others to act** when the girls practice various ways to get their message across to people in their neighborhood to SAVE water by checking for leaks.

- Assist the girls as they get organized to work on whatever might be needed for their SAVE effort—signs, booklets, a skit, etc.

When volunteers assist girls with their SAVE projects by helping them organize their efforts, that's **Girl Led** at the Brownie grade level. Girls at this age are able to take the lead on decision-making, but they might need help carrying out their plans.

- Or invite the girls to talk with a special visitor whose work or volunteer effort is related to the Brownie Team's SAVE project. For example, perhaps someone from the local water utility.

When girls seek out community members to get more information on a topic of their choice, or to partner with them on a Take Action project such as their SAVE effort, they are moving toward the **Connect outcome of Girls feel connected to their communities, locally and globally.**

As the Brownies plan their effort, guide them to promote good teamwork by:

- Encouraging them to take turns
- Making sure each girl has a role
- Praising girls when you observe great cooperation

BE KIND TO WATER!

This section is an excellent example of the **Connect outcome, Girls promote cooperation and team-building.** As Brownies work together on their SAVE projects, they start to fine-tune their cooperation and team-building skills. All of this is achieved through the **Cooperative Learning** process, as girls work together on the common goal of their SAVE project.

Snapshot of the Junior Journey

SESSION 1	**Start Your Engines** Juniors begin to experience the various forms of energy and how they can make the most of their own energy to conserve Earth's energy. They get an overview of the journey and its prestigious leadership awards, discuss the basics of energy efficiency, make recycled paper, and name their unique personal energy.
SESSION 2	**Pledging to Save Energy** Juniors commit to an energy pledge, take a look at how plants use energy, and sort through some of the wasted energy they see around them—all activities leading to the Energize Award. They also consider a Team Energy Pledge, assess the waste in excess packaging, make beads from recycled paper, and consider how leaders use energy.
SESSION 3	**Get Wild About Energy (and How to Conserve It)** Juniors investigate how animals use energy according to their needs and consider what humans might learn from them. They also compare and contrast animal and human communication strategies.
SESSION 4	**Investigating Buildings** Juniors begin to explore energy use in buildings as they delve deeper into the science of energy and get ready to conduct an energy audit of a community building.
SESSIONS 5 & 6	**The Energy Audit** The Juniors conduct an energy audit of a community building and then educate and inspire others about the importance of energy efficiency as they move toward their Investigate Award.
SESSION 7	**Gearing Up to Go** The Juniors begin thinking about their Innovate project. They discuss various project ideas, learning interviewing techniques, talk about their ideas for energizing food choices, and make silhouettes.
SESSION 8	**Moving in New Directions** The Juniors move toward a team decision on an Innovate project. Depending on the girls' interest, they may conduct a walkability/bikeability survey of their community, and then make a team decision on their project.
SESSIONS 9 & 10	**Innovate!** The Juniors plan and carry out their Innovate project, taking action to create changes in energy use on Earth, and educating and inspiring others along the way. The girls also check on their teamwork and conflict-resolution strategies.
SESSION 11	**Crossing the Finish Line** The Juniors reflect on and celebrate their accomplishments along the journey, earn the Innovate Award, and look ahead to more energizing adventures in Girl Scouting.

NATIONAL LEADERSHIP OUTCOMES

		AT THE JUNIOR LEVEL, girls...	RELATED ACTIVITIES (by session number or girls' book section/page)	SAMPLE "SIGN" When the outcome is achieved, girls might...
DISCOVER	Girls develop a strong sense of self.	gain a clearer sense of their individual identities.	S1: Personal Energy	report increased confidence in dealing with outside pressures.
	Girls develop positive values.	gain greater understanding of ethical decision making in their lives.	S1: Making Recycled Paper. GB: Energy-Saving Adventure, p. 21, Recycled Paper, pp. 36-39	give examples of using the Girl Scout Promise and Law in deciding to "do what's right."
		have increased commitment to engage in sustainable community service and action.	S2, S4: Opening Ceremonies. GB: Carbon Footprint, pp. 16-17; Energy Pledge, pp. 18-20; Weighing Waste, p. 32; Energy Award, p. 106; Moving Right Along, pp. 111-112	feel it's important to help people and the environment in ways that will have a long-term positive impact.
	Girls gain practical life skills.	gain greater understanding of what it means to be emotionally and physically healthy.	Energy Snacks, adult guide, p. 30. GB: Any Bean Soup, p. 23; Walking Salad, p. 31	describe how being stressed can affect physical health.
	Girls seek challenges in the world.	increasingly recognize that positive risk-taking is important to personal growth and leadership.	S2: Energy Pledge; S4: Opening Ceremony; S5, S6: Communicate with Style; S7: Lightbulbs	when asked to identify attitudes important to accomplishing goals, mention risk-taking and give examples from their own lives.
		are better at exploring new skills and ideas.	S1: Recycled Paper; S2: Plants, Light; S3: Observing Animals, Animal Energy Movement; S4, S5, S6: Energy Audit. GB: Kinetic and Potential Energy, pp. 10-12; You Unplugged, pp. 14-17; Wasted Energy, pp. 44-49; Energy Insights, pp. 52-59; Recycled Paper, pp. 36-39; Energy Audit, pp. 68-75; On the Move, pp. 76-79; Investigate Award, p. 107	report using a variety of resources to pursue topics of interest.
CONNECT	Girls promote cooperation and team building.	increasingly recognize how cooperation contributes to a project's success.	S5, S6: Communication Maze; S7: Thinking About a Team Choice	consistently prefer solving problems in teams or as a group and explain why this can be more effective than working alone.
	Girls feel connected to their communities.	begin to feel part of a larger community of girls/women.	GB: Profiles of women/girls, pp. 22, 24-25, 34-35, 40-43, 50, 51, 67, 83, 84	enjoy connecting with girls/women locally, nationally, or globally.
	Girls develop healthy relationships.	strengthen communication skills for maintaining healthy relationships.	S3: Relate and Communicate!; S5, S6: Relate and Communicate: Favorite Tips	name communication strategies that help them in their relationships.
TAKE ACTION	Girls can identify community needs.	learn to use strategies to determine issues that deserve action.	S8: Walkability/Biking Checklist	use community asset mapping to identify opportunities to better their communities.
	Girls are resourceful problem solvers.	are better able to create an "action plan" for their projects.	S5, S6: How Does Your Building Stack Up?; S8: Innovate Project; S9, S10: Planning Time: Innovate; GB: An Innovative Idea, pp. 80-81; Innovate Award, pp. 108-109	outline steps, resources, and time lines and assign responsibilities for their project with minimal adult guidance.
		gain a greater ability to locate and use resources that will help accomplish their project goals.	S5, S6: Energy Audit; S7: How to Conduct an Interview. GB: An Innovative Idea, p. 35; Innovate Award, pp. 108-109	feel confident contacting community partners who can help them achieve their goals.
	Girls advocate for themselves and others.	strengthen their abilities to effectively speak out or act for themselves and others.	S4-S10: Investigate and Innovate projects; S5, S6: Speak Up for Change. GB: Investigate, p. 107	identify concrete steps they can take to effect desired changes.
	Girls educate and inspire others to act.	learn various strategies to communicate and share Take Action Projects with others.	S2: How Leaders Energize; S5, S6: Speak Up for Change; S11: Celebrate	use various ways to tell others about their Take Action Projects.
			S2: Team Strand of Beads; S3: Communication Dos and Don'ts; S5, S6: Communicate with Style	explain what makes a successful persuasive message/action for various audiences.
	Girls feel empowered to make a difference.	are more confident in their power to effect positive change.	S7: Lightbulbs	describe various expressions of power around them.
		feel they have greater opportunities for involvement in the decision making of their communities.	S11 Reflecting on the Journey. GB: Innovate Award, pp. 107-108; Celebrate, p. 112	explain how shared power helped them create better or longer-lasting changes.

S=Session, GB=Girls' Book

Seeing Processes and Outcomes Play Out in *GET MOVING!*

Girl Scout processes play out in a variety of ways during team gatherings, but often they are so seamless you might not notice them. For example, in Session 3 (page 44), the Juniors go out into nature to observe animals in their natural habitat. The call-outs below show how the Girl Scout processes and outcomes make this activity a learning and growing experience for girls—and up the fun, too! Throughout *GET MOVING!*, you'll see processes and outcomes play out again and again. Before you know it, you'll be using these valuable aspects of Girl Scouting in whatever Juniors do—from planning a camping trip to earning the Girl Scout Bronze Award.

FROM SAMPLE SESSION 3

GET WILD ABOUT ENERGY (AND HOW TO CONSERVE IT)

Opening Ceremony

Since they're gathering at a special place to observe animals in nature, the girls might form a circle and name one hope they have for their outing today.

Observing Animals in Their Natural Setting

If you and the girls have arranged to get out in nature to observe animals, this is the time to do it! Encourage the girls to jot their thoughts, notes, and drawings of all that they see and hear and smell.

If your group isn't out in nature, viewing a nature movie or some nature shows on TV (or taped from TV) are good options. The girls can observe the animals and then follow the same discussion points and activities.

> This is an example of the **Girl Led** process. Opening ceremonies should always be Girl Led, with girls taking the lead on conducting the ceremony. At the Junior grade level, the girls can determine how to modify ceremonies to suit their interests.

> This is a good example of **Learning by Doing.** Girls are going out in nature and observing animals for themselves, rather than watching someone else do it or just reading about it. There is an added element of complexity and benefit for the girls when they record their observations and thoughts, perhaps for later use. This could also relate to the **Discover outcome, Girls seek challenges in the world,** since the Juniors are going out and exploring the world and their thoughts and ideas.

This section is an excellent example of the adult-girl partnership in the **Girl Led** process. The adult volunteer is guiding the girls in a discussion by asking them pointed questions about their experiences and observations. The "W and H questions" (who, what, when, where, why, how) are especially useful for getting the ball rolling for a discussion with younger girls.

Animals, Energy, and Movement

After the girls have finished their allotted time for observing animals, guide them in a discussion about what they've seen. Here are some questions you might ask to get them started:

- *What sort of animal energy and animal movement did you see today?*

- *How is movement necessary to an animal's survival?*

- *How do animals use sound energy?*

- *How do humans use the energy of animals?*

- *Did you read about the phrase "charismatic megafauna" from the story about the scientist who studies elephants in your book? Why do you think we like certain animals enough to try to protect them?*

While this question is part of the "W and H questions" noted above, it also serves another purpose: moving the girls toward achieving the **Discover outcome, Girls develop critical thinking**. It is asking girls to take information they have gathered and use it to explain a complex idea, such as the reasoning behind protecting animals.

PETS ARE ANIMALS, TOO

Steer the girls into a related discussion about energy and the animals they're likely to be most familiar with: pets. To get them going, pose a few questions, such as:

- *Do cats or dogs or other pets get as much chance as deer or prairie dogs or other wild animals to run around and move freely?*

- *What happens when pets don't get to use their energy properly?*

- *How can people make sure pets get enough exercise?*

- *Do you notice how exercising a pet gets you some exercise, too?*

In addition to being an "H question" to get girls thinking about the health of pets, this could also be the preliminary question for moving toward the **Take Action outcome, Girls are resourceful problem solvers**. It's asking girls to gather their existing resources to find a solution to the problem of pets needing more exercise.

This last question, though it requires only a yes or no answer, gets girls to start thinking about different ways to stay healthy, which is the **Discover outcome, Girls gain practical life skills**.

85

Snapshot of the Cadette Journey

SESSION 1 — **Blare in the Air!** Girls focus on the sense of hearing as they explore both the noise people routinely create and the sounds of silence and nature. They begin to consider how what they value influences how they care for Earth's air. They also reflect on the importance of making silent time for themselves.

SESSION 2 — **Scent Sense** Girls explore how various scents make them feel. They begin to consider relaxation techniques, and why their AWAREness of air matters.

SESSION 3 — **What's in the Air?** Girls investigate the science of air. They use what they've learned to create an air-quality observation tool and deepen their AWAREness of the importance of caring for air.

SESSION 4 — **Get AWARE** Girls observe and record air-quality issues at their chosen location. They consider the flair each girl brings to the team, and their reasons for caring about air.

SESSION 5 — **ALERT Who About What?** Girls earn their AWARE Awards and share their personal reason for caring about air. They make a team choice about an ALERT project to engage others in caring for air.

SESSION 6 — **Inspiration, Please!** Girls plan the specifics of their ALERT project, including identifying an Air Care Team and choosing how they will influence the team to act for air.

SESSION 7 — **ALERT! It's Happening!** Girls put their ALERT project in motion by using what they know to educate and inspire an Air Care Team to act.

SESSION 8 — **Take the Pulse** Girls earn their ALERT Awards and consider the impact of their efforts. They develop ideas to AFFIRM the results of their actions and enjoy "Air Time" activities.

SESSION 9 — **Signs of AFFIRMation** Girls create their AFFIRMation collage and a note about it for Girl Scout Juniors. They earn the AFFIRM Award, and plan their celebration.

SESSION 10 — **Up, Up, and Away!** Girls celebrate their accomplishments on this journey and as Heirs Apparent of air and all Earth's elements.

NATIONAL LEADERSHIP OUTCOMES

		AT THE CADETTE LEVEL, girls...	RELATED ACTIVITIES (by session number or girls' book page)	SAMPLE "SIGN" When the outcome is achieved, girls might...
DISCOVER	Girls develop a strong sense of self.	show an increase in self-efficacy.	GB: Flair, p. 49	report increased belief in their ability to achieve personal goals.
	Girls develop positive values.	are better able to examine their own and others' values from individual, cultural, and global perspectives.	GB: Profiles of women and girls; Aware Award, pp. 104–105	report greater appreciation for the diversity of values based on individual and/or cultural differences.
	Girls gain practical life skills—girls practice healthy living.	are increasingly committed to practicing and promoting healthy behavior.	S2: Scent Sense; S3: Relaxed. GB: Music to Your Ears? Noise, Noise Level, pp. 20–25; Need Some Space, pp. 27 and 77; Elevate Your Air Power, p. 75	report increased interest in learning more about how exercise, diet, relaxation, and other activities can give balance to their lives.
CONNECT	Girls develop healthy relationships.	are able to use positive communication and relationship-building skills.	GB: Air It Out, p. 30.	give examples of behaviors they use to promote mutual respect, trust, and understanding.
	Girls promote cooperation and team building.	have a greater understanding of team building.	S6: Adding Our Flair; S7: Team Check	list criteria for what makes a good team (e.g., clear roles, trust, respect, diversity).
		are better able to address obstacles to effective group work and team building.	S8: Pulse Check Teamwork	describe obstacles to group work (e.g., not being willing to compromise, concern with individual interests over group goals, always wanting to be the person talking) and suggest possible solutions.
	Girls feel connected to their communities, locally and globally.	strengthen existing relationships and seek to create new connections with others in their communities.	S6: Sounding the Call. GB: Alert, pp. 106–108	feel more confident contacting community members for help with community service and action projects (e.g., teachers, youth organizations, after-school clubs).
TAKE ACTION	Girls can identify community needs.	strengthen their ability to decide which community issue deserves action.	S4: Get Aware Observational Trip; S5: Observing the Observations. GB: Compare Air log, pp. 14–15; No Idling Zone, pp. 44–45; Get Out in the Air and Permanent Paper Reduction, p. 63; What's in Your Air?, p. 67	report using a variety of tools (e.g., community mapping, interviewing, observations) to identify needs, assets, and potential impact of their planned projects.
	Girls are resourceful problem solvers.	are able to create and implement detailed action plans for their projects.	S3: Planning for Air Care Field Observation; S5: Choosing an Alert; S7: Planning and Conducting a Meeting	demonstrate independence in thinking through required components of their action plans (e.g., location of resources, time lines, responsibilities).
		increasingly seek out community support and resources to help achieve their goals.	S6: Identifying the Air Care Team; S7, S8: ALERT Award	identify people/organizations in their communities to help on some aspect of their project.
	Girls advocate for themselves and others, locally and globally.	recognize the importance of advocacy in accomplishing positive changes for themselves and others.	S8: Gathering Some Affirmations	give examples of how youth can influence and/or participate in community decision making (e.g., influence the library to remain open longer, start a teen hotline, form an antidiscrimination group).
	Girls educate and inspire others to act.	show increased commitment to educate others on how to better their communities.	S9: Opening Ceremony: Affirm	organize a show-and-tell for younger Girl Scouts to educate them about how to be more active in community affairs.

S=Session, GB=Girls' Book

Seeing Processes and Outcomes Play Out in *Breathe*

Girl Scout processes play out in a variety of ways during team gatherings, but often they are so seamless you might not notice them. For example, in Session 4 (pages 60–61), the Cadettes take part in an air-quality Observational Field Trip that sets the stage for their ALERT project. The call-outs below show how the Girl Scout processes make the ceremony at the close of this activity a learning and growing experience for girls—and up the fun, too! Throughout *Breathe*, you'll see processes and outcomes play out again and again. Before you know it, you'll be using these valuable aspects of Girl Scouting in whatever Cadettes do—from going for the Girl Scout Silver Award to participating in Girl Scout Cookie Activities!

> This is a nice transition out of the cycle of action and reflection in the **Learning by Doing** process and right into **Girl Led**. As the girls reflect on their air observations—perhaps through the writing of the personal statement itself—they get to know themselves and their values a little better. This progression is building toward a combination of the Cadette-level **Discover outcomes, Girls develop a strong sense of self** and **Girls develop positive values**. And as girls gain expertise in their own feelings and beliefs, they are able to express what they've learned for the benefit of themselves and the group. This expression is **Girl Led**.

FROM SAMPLE SESSION 4

Get AWARE

Closing Ceremony

Let the team know that they have made excellent progress toward earning their AWARE awards—and perhaps even completed all the steps! Encourage the team to check out the steps on the Award Tracker on pages 102–103 of their book. What do they have left to do? If they have not yet talked to some experts, what ideas do they have about doing so?

Note that the last step to earning AWARE is for each girl to write a personal statement about why she cares about air, one that she will share with the rest of the team. The girls can do this now, as their closing, or opt to do so at the opening of their next gathering.

If they need a little assistance to get going, ask a few questions, like these:

- *What have you become more aware of related to air in our lives since Breathe started?*

Can you imagine being an au pair and taking a pair of toddlers out into the fresh air?

These questions help girls learn more about their values and beliefs regarding air quality, and they are also specifically about people's health. This ties to the **Discover outcome, Girls gain practical life skills—girls practice healthy living**. At the Cadette grade level, the girls' reflection upon this issue shows their commitment to promoting healthy behavior.

- *What matters to you: Making more quiet time to tune into ourselves and nature? Dealing with the source of smells that are bad for us to breathe in? Trying to prevent kids from smoking? Making sure we have more plants and trees?*

- *Why do these things matter to you? Why be AWARE and care?*

- *Isn't it interesting how what is good for Earth is good for us, too?*

Consider also using the closing today to engage girls in thinking about all the interesting education and career possibilities available to them. There are so many to gain AWAREness of!

Suggest they flip through their book for a few minutes and select their favorite from among the women and girls doing something for Earth. Then, ask the girls to say a few words about what new possibilities the story makes them AWARE of and why they are intrigued. You can do this as a large group or in small teams.

In addition to thinking about the women featured in their book, girls could also think about what they have learned from any guests they have networked with during *Breathe* gatherings, or stories they are AWARE of in the news.

This is the **Cooperative Learning** process. Girls team up, either in small groups or one large one, to share their thoughts and ideas on their new awareness of environmental careers.

Ceremonies should be **Girl Led**. Though the volunteer suggests that girls flip through their book, it is the girl who decides which woman most appeals to her.

The reading and thinking the girls are asked to do here opens them up to a range of women doing good for the planet. In their choice of a favorite female leader, they must first assess (consciously or unconsciously) their own values. This moves them toward the **Discover outcome, Girls develop positive values.**

This activity also relates to the **Connect outcome, Girls feel connected to their community, locally and globally.** The women and girls featured in their book give the Cadettes a sense of belonging to a community of women and girls working in support of the environment.

Snapshot of the Senior Journey

SESSION 1	**So What About Sow What?** The Seniors become aware of their place in the global food network as they start to think about where food really comes from and how their choices about food impact Planet Earth. They begin to customize their *Sow What?* journey in order to make a real difference in the food network.
SESSION 2	**Foraging for Food!** The Seniors explore the food network in their communities and gather ideas, information, and contacts they can use as they think about how to improve their involvement in the food network.
SESSION 3	**What Makes a Meal Really Happy?** The Seniors explore the pleasures of the "local harvest" as they consider all the "ingredients" that go into a truly happy meal. They then compare this experience to some of their day-to-day encounters with food and the food network. They also think about what makes relationships nourishing.
SESSION 4	**Dig Deeper** The Seniors investigate local agricultural practices and find out what some of the challenges are for people who produce food in their region and for the larger food network. The girls also compare soil samples, and consider a range of options, from learning about food connections in their families to the waste-saving benefits of composting.
SESSION 5	**Sow What?: Global Outlook** The Seniors focus their attention on the global issue of hunger, considering how their own decisions and actions impact the food network around the world. The girls also consider the values represented by the various women featured in their books and how they and these women are connected. They also share their gratitude for the food and nurturing they have in their lives.
SESSION 6	**Planning to Harvest** The Seniors identify their project for the Harvest Award. The girls check in on their commitments and their teamwork, and consider the importance of advocacy in their project.
SESSIONS 7 & 8	**Harvest Time!** The Seniors team up and carry out their efforts to have a positive impact on the food network, en route to earning their Harvest Awards. They also consider career opportunities, assess healthy relationships, and create a food ceremony or festival.
SESSIONS 9 & 10	**Reap What You Sow!** The Seniors conclude their *Sow What?* journey, assessing what they have learned, connecting with all those who have assisted them, and celebrating their Harvest. The girls also share their Harvest projects and see if any ideas emerge about keeping the effort going.

NATIONAL LEADERSHIP OUTCOMES

		AT THE SENIOR LEVEL, girls...	RELATED ACTIVITIES (by session number or girls' book part/page)	SAMPLE "SIGN" When the outcome is achieved, girls might...
DISCOVER	Girls develop a strong sense of self.	are better able to recognize the multiple demands and expectations of others while establishing their own individuality.	S7, S8: Career Possibilities	describe challenges they face in finding a balance between accepting group beliefs and thinking/making decisions for themselves.
	Girls develop positive values.	strengthen their own and others' commitment to being socially, politically, and environmentally engaged citizens of their communities.	S3: So What Can You Commit To?. GB: Count Your Kernels, p. 45; Your Own BioBlitz, p. 49; So, What About Values?, p. 85	report increased positive attitudes of social responsibility and citizenship.
	Girls gain practical life skills—girls practice healthy living.	show cultural sensitivity in their efforts to promote healthy living in their communities.	S1: The Real Food Network; S2: Food Forage; S3: Hunger Pains; S7–S8: Harvest project	report increased knowledge of specific health needs in their diverse communities.
	Girls seek challenges in the world.	demonstrate increased enthusiasm for learning new skills and ideas and expanding existing ones.	S2: Food Forage; S3: Agricultural Visit; Harvest Project	increasingly offer their own ideas for exploring new topics or making existing ones more challenging.
	Girls develop critical thinking.	are better able to analyze their own and others' thinking processes.	S1: The Real Food Network; S5: Hunger Pain	give examples of the steps they followed and why they made a specific decision or formed an opinion.
CONNECT	Girls develop healthy relationships.	are better able to recognize and address challenges to forming and maintaining healthy relationships with others.	S2, S3, S7, S8	identify behaviors that hinder the development of positive relationships (e.g., backstabbing, gossip).
	Girls promote cooperation and team building.	strengthen their abilities to build effective teams to accomplish shared goals.	S7, S8: Harvest Project Checklist	identify specific strategies for building effective teams (e.g., paying attention to interests, strengths, team dynamics).
	Girls feel connected to their communities, locally and globally.	feel that their connections with diverse members of their communities are important resources for personal and leadership development.	S5: Shared Values, Hunger Pain. GB: All profiles of women and girls	make friends with girls/women through the World Association of Girl Guides and Girl Scouts and can explain why these connections are important to them.
TAKE ACTION	Girls can identify community needs.	are more skilled in identifying their local or global communities' needs that they can realistically address.	S2: Food Forage. GB: Harvest Award Topics, pp. 89–92	report considering multiple factors before deciding on the appropriateness of a project for their community.
			S7, S8: Who Can You Meet?, Power of More. GB: Cultivate Network, p. 88	seek advice from community members/leaders before selecting issues for action.
	Girls advocate for themselves and others.	have a greater understanding of how the decisions and policies of various institutions have effects on their lives and the lives of others.	S9, S10: Harvest Project Award. GB: Harvest Project, pp. 86–95	report increased knowledge about how public decisions in their schools, communities, and local governments affect people's private lives.
		use advocacy skills and knowledge to be more active on behalf of a cause, issue, or person, locally or globally.		give examples of advocating for an issue in their school or neighborhood.
	Girls educate and inspire others to act.	are better at inspiring and mobilizing others to become more engaged in community service and action.	Harvest Project; S10: Harvest Time: Leader Prints. GB: Make It Official, p. 87	shape messages (e.g., in a flier, speech, publication, or Web campaign) to explain the importance of taking action on an issue they care about.
	Girls feel empowered to make a difference.	feel that they have greater access to community resources and more equal relationships with adults in their communities.	S9, S10: Harvest Project Award. GB: Harvest Project, pp. 86–95	report that adults in their communities invite their input and/ or participation in community affairs.

S=Session, GB=Girls' Book

Seeing Processes and Outcomes Play Out in *Sow What?*

irl Scout processes play out in a variety of ways during team gatherings, but often they are so seamless you might not notice them. For example, in Session 1, the Seniors take part in a food network exercise (pages 35–36) that gets them thinking about how their food choices impact the planet. The call-outs below show how the Girl Scout processes make this a learning and growing experience for girls—and up the fun, too! Throughout *Sow What?*, you'll see processes and outcomes play out again and again. Before you know it, you'll be using these valuable aspects of Girl Scouting in whatever Seniors do—from going for the Girl Scout Silver Award to going on a trip to participating in Girl Scout Cookie Activities!

AMP IT UP

Depending on the mood and energy of the girls and time available, they might like to add humor or drama by turning this into a guessing game or even a "mini-commercial" about their good favorites. If the team wants to get creative, they might enjoy spending a few minutes preparing their "performance."

This is **Girl Led** with pizzazz! Besides taking the lead in presenting their ideas, they get to put a creative spin on it, making it informative and entertaining!

FROM SAMPLE SESSION 1

The Real Food Network

Now it's time for the girls to begin to envision all the resources—Earth's resources and people resources—as well as all the various decisions about those resources, that bring food to their tables. Invite girls to explore where their favorites they've named "come from" (besides the store!).

Start by asking: *How many people, animals, and resources of Earth—the sun, water, and air—go into getting our food to us?*

Ask the girls to choose a favorite food they've talked about today (or one ingredient in a food) and then tell the story of the web of interactions that brings that food to their table. They can make educated guesses or simply use their imaginations. But they must tell a whole story. You might say:

> *Start with what the sun did for it or what water did for it and move forward through all the steps that let this food reach its final destination—you!*

As the girls think about the world's resources, how people get them, and who gets to use them, they build toward the **Discover outcome, Girls develop critical thinking.** They also begin to gain a greater understanding of how these decisions and policies affect people's lives. This is a key element of the Senior-level **Take Action outcome, Girls advocate for themselves and others, locally and globally.**

Girls working together to figure out the path food takes to get to them is a good example of **Cooperative Learning**. This activity also has girls making the connection between "local" (their communities) and "global." This is most closely aligned with the **Connect outcome, Girls feel connected to their communities, locally and globally.**

The girls might like to do this individually, in mini-teams, or as a large team. They can keep their examples simple—and have some fun, creatively capturing the story/web on a piece of paper or two. To get their stories going, ask them to consider questions like these, that get them thinking through the a full "food time line":

Say your favorite food is an orange. Who planted the seed that became the orange tree? Who decided what kind of seed to plant and how? Where? Maybe in Florida? Who tended the tree? Was it treated with pesticides? Fertilizers? Artificial or natural? Who decided? Where did that stuff come from? When the tree produced fruit, who picked it? Who tasted it? Packed it? Shipped it? Who unloaded it at the store? Priced it? Displayed it for you? Who bought it? How does it taste?

Invite each girl or team of girls to share her/their food network story. Then, guide a short discussion:

- *How does our food connect us to Earth?*
- *How does our food connect us to people?*
- *When you bite into a piece of food, do you ever think about the people who produce it, pick it, or deliver it to you? Do you ever wonder whether they actually eat this food themselves?*
- *What are some of the decisions that get made along our food networks? How do they impact people and the planet?*
- *What ideas are we starting to have about how decisions along our food networks impact health—the health of the environment and our own?*

Encourage the girls to research, before the next gathering, more facts on their own to learn how close to the truth their network stories really come. Did they leave out any links in the web? Did they leave out any key people?

These guiding questions lead girls to the **Discover outcome, Girls develop positive values**. They ask girls to go beyond technical or scientific explanations to think about the social and political aspects of food. As they grapple with the answers, the girls may "strengthen their own and others' commitment to being socially, politically and environmentally engaged citizens" in their communities, locally and globally.

This question focuses on the **Discover outcome, Girls gain practical life skills—girls practice healthy living.** It asks girls to consider healthy living as it pertains to their own lives and the environment. It also asks them to think about food in a global context, and from social and cultural perspectives. This is an important and challenging aspect of this outcome for Seniors—"girls show cultural sensitivity in their efforts to promote healthy living in their communities."

This encouragement is part of the adult-girl partnership in the **Girl Led** process. The adult volunteer encourages the girls to confirm or rethink their thoughts through research. This supports the girls in building toward the **Discover outcome, Girls seek challenges in the world**.

Snapshot of the Ambassador Journey

SESSION 1	**Toward Justice** The Ambassadors begin to think about what justice asks of each of us as individuals. They examine the ways in which environmental concerns can be ranked based on various needs and perspectives. They go on to explore how desires for justice compete with self-interests.
SESSION 2	**Look High, Look Wide** The Ambassadors find ways to see the big picture of environmental justice issues. They explore what it means to "sit at every stone," and consider how a "high and wide" perspective can help resolve personal conflicts.
SESSION 3	**Do the Math** The Ambassadors identify ways to lighten their step on the planet and make a commitment to follow through and record their results. They explore how Doing the Math can be an effective motivation tool in the quest for environmental justice.
SESSION 4	**Be Hawk-Eyed** The Ambassadors sharpen their critical eye for environmental issues by learning to look beyond the hype. They also consider how getting the facts can be a good strategy for conflict resolution.
SESSION 5	**Take the Scientific View** The Ambassadors investigate the role of science and uncertainty in environmental justice issues by interviewing scientists.
SESSION 6	**Decipher Decisions** The Ambassadors explore the complexity of decision making when various needs compete. Ultimately, they develop ideas about "just decision making" to add to their growing equations for justice.
SESSION 7	**What's the Equation?** The Ambassadors create their definition and equation for justice, and choose the audience for their presentation. They also consider "new equations" for themselves as they talk about career options along their journey.
SESSION 8	**Who Will Listen?** The Ambassadors continue to plan their presentation to define justice and share an equation for achieving it.
SESSION 9	**Inspiring Justice** The Ambassadors share their vision of justice—what it means and how we get it—with others and invite everyone to make strides toward justice by Doing the Math. Following their presentation, girls take time to talk through everything they've explored along the journey.
SESSION 10	**Celebrate!** The Ambassadors reflect on what they have learned along their journey toward justice, enjoy a closing celebration, and take a look at how they might continue their pursuit of justice.

NATIONAL LEADERSHIP OUTCOMES

		AT THE AMBASSADOR LEVEL, girls...	RELATED ACTIVITIES (by session number or girls' book page)	SAMPLE "SIGN" When the outcome is achieved, girls might...
DISCOVER	Girls develop a strong sense of self.	feel they are better equipped to pursue future/life goals.	S4, S7, S9	report that they have options and possibilities for life/career goals.
	Girls develop positive values.	act consistently with a considered and self-determined set of values.	S3: Guilty Habits, Math; S4: Math; S6: I Changed My Mind, Check the Math; S8: Check the Math. GB: Hot on Campus, pp. 90–91	choose educational and career goals in line with the values they consider important.
		demonstrate commitment to promoting sustainable solutions to problems.	S1: Opening, Simple List; S2: Start Your E; S4, S5, S6: Add It In; S8: Opening. GB: Hearts & Minds; and pp. 9, 15–16, 22–23, 46; 47–49, 69, and 101	report increased interest in making a sustainable impact beyond their local communities.
	Girls seek challenges in the world.	increasingly set challenging goals for the future.	S5: Opening Ceremony	see themselves in roles previously considered unattainable.
		have increased confidence to discuss and address challenging issues and contradictions in their lives and in their communities.	S1: Ranking; S2: Bird's-Eye; S3: Math; S4: Beyond the Hype; Get Dramatic; S5: Interviews; Whose Opinion; S6: Interview a DM. GB: pp. 38–41, 45–65	look for ways personal habits conflict with achieving goals.
			GB: pp. 17–19, 32–37	learn more about an issue from someone who has experienced injustice.
CONNECT	Girls promote cooperation and team building.	recognize the value of cooperation and team building for leadership and careers.	S1: Team Plans and Goals; S2: Casing It Out, Making Choices; S3: Opening, Closing; S8 Presentation Prep. GB: pp. 26, 55, 88, 96, and 99	report that cooperation and team-building skills helped them in other spheres of their lives.
	Girls feel connected to their communities.	have extensive feelings of connection with their local and global communities.	S3: Surveying; S7, S8: Opening Ceremony. GB: Karen Panetta feature, p. 8; Look High, Look Wide, p. 25	report more positive attitudes toward different members of their communities.
	Girls can resolve conflicts.	are better able to develop their own approaches to conflict resolution	S4, S9	give examples of how they adapted conflict-resolution strategies to personal situations.
TAKE ACTION	Girls can identify community needs.	are more skilled in identifying issues that balance feasibility with long-term change.	S2: Map It Out; S3: Surveying; S4: Survey Says	identify community partners that can continue their project goals into the future.
		choose projects that aim to address deeper causes of issues in their communities.	S6: Tracking the Footprint of a Decision	interview staff and residents of a shelter to identify root causes of homelessness in the community.
	Girls are resourceful problem solvers.	are better able to independently plan, organize, and manage projects.	S5: Controversy Strikes; S6: Interview a Decision Maker; S7: The E; S8: Presentation Prep. GB: Toward the Sage, pp. 10–13; Start, Continue, and Add to Your E, pp. 43, 92, and 102	monitor their own progress and determine criteria for success.
	Girls advocate for themselves and others.	recognize they can take part in development of public policy.	S5: Whose Opinion Really Counts?	report increased interest in projects that promote positive social changes.
		seek partnerships with groups that aid advocacy efforts.	S7: Who Cares?	report working with organizations that share their advocacy goals.
	Girls educate and inspire others to act.	are better able to evaluate the effectiveness of their efforts to educate diverse audiences.	S3: Math, Add to the E; S7: E, Who Cares? S8: Tips; S10: Reflection. GB: Nest, p. 70; Tips, pp. 106–108	implement innovative ways to access hard-to-reach audiences.
			S7: Reaching Out. GB: Do the Math, p. 45	work with other organizations to spread their messages effectively.
	Girls feel empowered to make a difference.	feel capable of bettering the functioning of communities.	GB: Where Will You Take Your E?, p. 109	create an action plan that could include more young people in setting town priorities.
		feel their projects and ideas are valued.	S9: Inspiring Justice; S10: Sage Award	give examples of positive reports about their Take Action Projects.

S=Session; GB=Girls' book; Math=Do the Math; E=Equation; DM=Decision-Maker; ECs= Environmental Citizens

Seeing Processes and Outcomes Play Out in *JUSTICE*

Girl Scout processes play out in a variety of ways during team gatherings, but often they are so seamless you might not notice them. For example, in Session 2, the Ambassadors map out a local environmental justice issue by taking a birds-eye view. The call-outs below show how the Girl Scout processes make this a learning and growing experience for girls—and up the fun, too! Throughout *JUSTICE*, you'll see processes and outcomes play out again and again. Before you know it, you'll be using these valuable aspects of Girl Scouting in whatever Ambassadors do—from going for the Girl Scout Gold Award to traveling abroad to participating in Girl Scout Cookie Activities!

FROM SAMPLE SESSION 2

Option: Map Out a Local Issue

The Ambassadors might want to dive in deeper to investigate a place or an emerging local issue, such as a landfill, factory, or power plant in their own region—by scoping out a birds-eye view.

The local news is a good place to start. Where is land being cleared to build something new? Who decided? Perhaps there are decisions pending that influence park lands or waste management. Girls can research the location of the problem and then map it in order to see where it is located with respect to residential and business neighborhoods. Who is being impacted? Who has not been involved in the decision? What LULUs and NIMBYs are in motion?

Encourage the Ambassadors to check out the Web site Scorecard.org, where they can type in their ZIP code and see how their county stacks up in terms of polluters, chemicals released, and industrial facilities. Is lead poisoning common in their community? Are there Superfund sites nearby? Scorecard allows the public to find out how much air pollution is released in their community, and how clean the water is in nearby rivers and lakes. It also provides environmental justice reports for the community.

This is an excellent example of girls focused on a **Take Action** outcome within the **Girl Led** process. Here, girls are determining which issue in their community is in need of attention. This is in line with the **Take Action outcome, Girls identify community needs.** Once they have determined the need, they engage in the **Girl Led** process to research the issue to get a better understanding of the underlying or "root cause" of the problem.

Here, through their research, girls are also starting to ask questions that challenge and expand their thinking prior to their investigation. This broad critical thinking is the focus of the **Discover outcome, Girls develop critical thinking skills,** and is at the heart of the "bird's-eye view" approach to issues!